IN EVERY
BELIEF IS A LIE

Copyright © 2022 by Lisa B. Schermerhorn

In Every Belief Is a Lie

Table of Contents

Thank you for purchasing my book, "In Every Belief is a Lie". As a special gift I have included videos of guided meditations and easy to learn techniques that you can do yourself to help you release your Lies.

If you enjoy this book,
please leave a review on amazon
and spread the word!.

Disclaimer

The information presented in "Every Belief is a Lie" is the author's opinion only and does not constitute any mental health or medical advice. The content of this book is for informational purposes only. This book is not intended to diagnose, treat, cure, or prevent any mental health condition or disease.

The ideas, suggestions, exercises, and techniques provided in this book are not intended as a substitute for seeking professional guidance. Please seek advice from your mental healthcare provider or healthcare provider for your personal health concerns prior to taking advice from this book.

The author shall not be held liable or responsible for any loss or damage allegedly arising from any suggestion or information contained in this book.

Dedication

A lifetime of learning and experiences have gone into writing this book. The following are people who made this book possible: my children, Max and Haylie. Without you, my life would have had little meaning.

To my teachers and dear friends, without your wisdom and tough love, I would not have had the tools to discover and release the Lies. A deep thank you and gratitude to my mother, Linda Friedman, my father, Ira Friedman, Manya Andersen, Rita Berkowitz, Karen Di Tripani, Steve Gamlin, Kevin Hoyt, Tracy Jaco, Michael Jaco, Yale Levey, Pat MacIsaac, Kevin Martin, Richard Messing, Aimee Mosco, Tucano Noni, Dr. Christiane Northrop, Karen Paolino-Correia, Corey Poirier, Ann Sousa, Christopher Salem, Lorianne Vaughan-Speaks, Shelley Kelley Sullivan, Dr. Al Tatarunus, Rhys Thomas, Janice Veech, Dahna Weber, Dr. Kimberlee Woods and my dear friend Rose Neves-Grigg. Without Rose's amazing healing abilities and wisdom, I would not be where I am now. www.rishikarose.com

A special thank you to Barrie Fisher for her extraordinary vision of my cover and her ability to capture the soul of this book. She is an incredibly talented photographer. To view her work, please go to www.barriefisherphoto.com.

Thank you to my ex-husband, Scott, who provided me with an opportunity to live an extraordinary life and raise two amazing children.

Deep gratitude to my guardian angel for keeping me on track and always believing in me.

Foreword

"In Every Belief Is a Lie"

I've always had a passion for shifting my belief systems while being an example and a resource to others for doing the same. It started over twenty-two years ago through a life-changing moment when my father was passing away from lung cancer. In hindsight, he was the source of my limiting belief—which was the need for validation from others—since I never received validation from him growing up. So when Lisa shared with me about her journey of discovering undisputed truth, it was so compelling that I knew it would inspire others on their journey to discovering their truth. Her passion for sharing and inspiring others by embracing their truth aligned so well with a journey I had been on for several years.

This passion for living my truth led me down a journey to being CEO of a 501c3 organization dedicated to creating an interdependent family structure for families free from limiting beliefs and eradicating codependency from generation to generation. This included serving business visionaries as a highly sought business executive coach, helping them to secure their "inner champion" and fulfill their purpose in business. I also wrote the international best–selling book *Master Your Inner Critic: Resolve the Root Cause Create Prosperity* with award-winning author Jack Canfield who wrote *Mastering the Art of Success*. I also am a radio show host to two leading shows called *Sustainable Success* with the Voice America Influencers Channel and *Business Influencers* with TalRadio.org, a division of the Touch-A-Life Foundation.

There are no coincidences about how Lisa and I met over a year ago. She was part of a speaker group I presented to on strategies and tactics to build their influence and obtain more speaking opportunities. She was so present and eager to learn. Her willingness to be transparent and vulnerable was compelling. I just knew she was going to share a powerful message to help others help themselves. This message would not just come through spoken word but also through print. Everyone reading this book will be glad they did as they embark on their journey.

Soon after this meeting, we began to work together. Lisa is a great listener and demonstrates an eagerness to learn and apply ideas that best help others through her personal and professional experience as a mindset expert. I considered it an honor when she reached out and asked me to provide the foreword to this work that will have a tremendous impact on people no matter where they are with their journey in life and business.

This book had been in the making for a long time with all the knowledge she has obtained studying Hypnosis, Neuro-Linguistic Programming (NLP), Shamanism, Energy Medicine, Emotional Freedom Technique (EFT), and the Emotional Release Technique. What will be most compelling to the others is her personal experience which clearly illustrates her journey with all the trials and tribulations in this book.

People will be taken on a journey to discover their own belief systems and how they were formed. They will learn how the lie is built, how the lies are confirmed, and how we inherit beliefs—the science of epigenetics. They will learn which tools best resonate with them so they can be used for releasing those beliefs that no longer serve them. Finally, they will understand how to replace those beliefs and manifest or create their dreams while discovering their undisputed truth.

First, let me say that I am a person that does not lend his name to just anyone who has not truly done the work to think, be, become, do, and have different and better results. Lisa is someone who has clearly done this and has committed her life to inspiring others through her example and resourcefulness. She lives her truth and has come to peace with her past. While she has twenty years of professional experience, as depicted earlier, it's her transparency through her story and personal experience that connects with others to evoke change. She has helped so many people from all areas of life to overcome their lies and uncover their undisputed truth. These people have embraced a journey like she did to be and become more than they ever imagined as part of the process.

I am honored again to recommend this book not just once but several times until it truly resonates at the deepest level in your soul. This process takes time and requires discipline and consistency on a daily basis to unpack the lies and begin living the truth that has always been inside of you. Every person willing to do the work with what this book shares will thank themselves they did. Reading this book is the start to a brand new chapter of change to enlighten your soul.

It's an honor again to be part of Lisa's journey through her book and her ability to help so many people that have struggled in silence. There has never been any hesitation working with her as she walks the talk while empowering others to take action over their belief systems from a place of empathy. This is a chance to give yourself permission to reclaim your truth and the belief system that will set you free from the bondage of limiting beliefs. This is your chance to experience true freedom to be you while becoming more to inspire others toward their process of doing the same.

To your health and prosperity.
Christopher R. Salem

Preface

I have been trying to write this book for twenty years. Every time I sat down to put words on the page, my mind would go blank. I also had some Lies I told myself—that what I had to say had already been said. Recently, I met a man named Richard Messing at an online networking group call. We connected over Zoom, and everything he said blew my mind. He asked me if I thought there should be more ethics in business, and I thought to myself, *Isn't that obvious?* He began to talk to me about his beliefs about free will and the case for human freedom. We discussed the importance of integrity and how our behavior needs to be consistent with our actions. We talked about the importance of trust by keeping your word so that you can create loyalty in your life and in your business.

Our beliefs are our perceptions, and our behavior is based on our perceptions. What if our perceptions are wrong? What if the lens through which we see the world is tainted or skewed? If our decisions and actions are based on that, how can we be in integrity? How do we know if we are actually acting of our own free will versus taking action based on being programmed by others?

I have worked with the subconscious mind since 2002, and I had never thought about our free will being related to ethics. It inspired me to investigate my own beliefs and how I came to my lens or view of the world. I realized that people might not fully understand where their beliefs come from, how their beliefs influence their lives, and that there are most likely Lies within their own beliefs.

What do I mean by Lies? Ten people can witness an event, and if you question each person individually, you will most likely get ten different stories of what happened. Why is that? Because we all come from different places and have had different experiences, our wounds all color how we see the world.

What if we could discern the Lie and find our actual Truth by releasing what really no longer serves us? The more you release the Lies, the happier and more authentic your life will be. The key is having the courage to honor your Truth. The first chapter is part of my story of how I found my Truth.

This book will take you on a journey of self-discovery. Find out where your Lies come from and learn some tools to release them. Everyone deserves an opportunity to live their life from a place of free will—the place where magic happens. When you live in your Truth, you will find joy in everything you do.

Introduction

In Every Belief Is a Lie

What would you do if you discovered that most of what you believe about yourself is a Lie? Did you know that you have spent most of your life programmed by your parents, teachers, friends, socioeconomic status, the news, culture, or religion? The list goes on.

In this book, you will discover all of the different ways you have been lied to, lied to yourself, and lied to others unconsciously. When you live a lie, it causes you to live your life in fear—you become stressed out and unhappy.

I have had a breadth of experience over the past twenty years, having had the opportunity to work as a vice president for an innovative start-up company, an entrepreneur in personal development, and an expert in the subconscious mind.

I invite you to take a journey with me to discover the different ways our brains absorb information, become programmed, and how we even inherit beliefs! I will offer you tools to release the Lies and help you unlock your Truth.

When you live a Lie, you live a life of fear and regret; you never reach your full potential. Living a Lie creates enormous amounts of stress and stress causes seventy percent of all disease.

Experience stories of self-discovery, exercises, guided meditations, and strategies for learning to live your Truth. The sooner you read this book, the sooner you are on your way to leaving the Lies behind, discovering your Truth, and living the life you have always dreamed of!

Chapter One

Into the Fire

I remember that day as if it were yesterday. I was standing in front of forty feet of red-hot, burning coals, saying to myself, *What was I thinking?*

In September of 2015, I found myself deeply depressed in a marriage of twenty-nine years that was no longer working. Both of my children were in college, and I was terrified to leave and be on my own. I felt trapped with no way out. One of my mentors, who was offering a training program on fire walk facilitation, contacted me. I was terrified of two things—being alone and walking on fire. I decided to take the fire walk facilitation course to conquer my fear of fire. I'd deal with the fear of being alone later.

The week-long training was grueling. It entailed breaking arrows with my throat, walking seven to ten feet of red-hot coals every night, walking on broken glass, and bending a ten-foot piece of rebar from my throat—I still have that piece of rebar. To graduate, the final was walking forty feet of red-hot coals.

Every night we reviewed and discussed that day's training, how it affected us, and what we needed to do to be better the next day. We would sit together and encourage and support each other as we walked our nightly seven to ten feet of red-hot coals, preparing for our final walk. I discovered that mindset was everything. If you are down and depressed, you should not walk on fire.

Everyone has qi energy, and the fire has its own qi energy. Your qi must be, at a minimum, as high as the fire's qi; otherwise, you will get burned. In order to walk on fire, you must feel strong, have joy, and have a high-energy vibration.

Tony Robbins is known for taking people through fire walks as part of his introductory program. He inspires people and pumps up their energy to get them in a confident and exuberant state of mind.

You would think that I was brave to take this on, but, as a matter of fact, I was the complete opposite, at least in my mind I was. As soon as I found out I needed to walk forty feet of fire, I went into a downward spiral, convinced that I was going to end up getting my feet burned, be in terrible pain, and end up in the emergency room in a hospital, having my feet amputated because they were so badly burned.

My poor classmates—I can't imagine what they had to endure with me in that program. I became a total whiny bitch. I cried, became a victim, felt sorry for myself, and often became inconsolable. When I think back on that experience, I realize that it was a metaphor for how I lived my life.

One of the many things that attracted me to my ex-husband was his fearlessness. He could talk me out of my fears and push me out of my comfort zone. This was something that I needed to learn to do for myself in order to push myself to the edge and venture into uncharted territories.

I grew up with undiagnosed learning disabilities and went to kindergarten a year early. I was the youngest in my class, and everyone could read, write, and do their numbers. I was lost. This began a cycle of years of feeling stupid, poor grades, spending every summer of my childhood in summer school, and getting in trouble for bad report cards. My self-esteem was very low, and I thought everyone was smarter than me. I gave my power away to anyone who I thought knew more than I did.

I married young, had two beautiful children, and, by the time I was in my mid-thirties, I had a breakdown; I felt lost. I found myself going from therapist to therapist, and I wasn't getting better. However, I was getting better at telling therapists what they wanted to hear because I wanted to be their best patient instead of really digging deep to find the root cause of my breakdown.

One day, a friend of mine suggested I go see a hypnotist. I exclaimed, "Hypno-what? Don't they make you quack like a duck?"

My friend laughed and said, "No, that's stage hypnotism. This is completely different. They will just speak to your subconscious mind, where all your memories are stored. You can't change what happened, but you can change the way you think about it— quickly."

I thought I had nothing to lose at that point, so I gave it a shot. I couldn't believe the difference in how I felt in such a short period of time. I was obsessed. I asked my hypnotist where she received her training because I wanted to be trained by all the people she trained with. She gave me a list of names to start with, and I could not stop studying. I finally found out that I was really good at something. I was actually really smart!

What I didn't realize was that because I didn't learn well in conventional settings and struggled with memorizing information, I was creative, artistic, and had the ability to solve problems. I can think outside the box. The more I studied, the more confidence I gained. Over the years, I earned a number of certifications, some of which include Certified Hypnotherapist, Master Practitioner in Neuro-Linguistic Programming, Reiki Master, Energy Medicine Practitioner, and Shamanic Practitioner. My insecurity about being stupid drove me to achieve and prove to myself and others that I am smart.

The problem was that I became smart in things that most of my friends and family didn't understand. I couldn't talk about what I had learned, and I found myself living a dual life, one of a conventional soccer Mom—or in my case, lacrosse Mom—and I also had a wellness center and private practice seeing clients. I didn't know what to call myself, let alone try and explain it to others. Marketing myself became a nightmare. My work was not mainstream and was too difficult for my ex-husband to understand.

To stay in our marriage, I tried to hide who I was until I couldn't hide it anymore. Depression set in. I was diagnosed with Lyme disease, and I had no energy for life. When my mentor asked me if I wanted to take the fire walking course, I thought, *Why not; I have nothing else to lose.*

I knew that I needed to face my fears. But what was I really afraid of? I realized that I was afraid to be me. Throughout my life, I had felt repeatedly rejected, and I didn't understand why people wanted to be around me. I was afraid to show up fully for fear of being ridiculed.

I remembered hearing a story of how eagles react when a storm is nearby. Instead of flying away from the storm, they fly directly into the storm. By flying into the storm, the winds lift the eagle up and raise it above the storm. Eagles are the only birds who do this. All other birds flee and hide. I find this an amazing metaphor for life. I now look at whatever I am afraid of and know that I must face it and walk towards it.

I came to realize that it was always fear of the fear I found paralyzing, not actually facing my fear. Every time I faced my fear, it amazed me how much easier it was than I thought it would be. Stepping into my fear has always brought me wisdom, courage, and a sense of accomplishment. I ended up realizing that the challenge in front of me was not as hard as I thought it would be. Something very powerful happens when we face our fears.

According to my friend and business partner Richard Messing, who founded the Kotel Business Group, which helps businesses solve their chronic human problems, "When we introduce a new experience that contradicts our beliefs about how to survive in the world, the contradiction indicates something is false, or the truth is missing, thus potentially harmful."[1]

Fear of this unknown compels us to seek the truth in order to survive the paradoxical situation in which we find ourselves. By freely choosing to face our fears, we create an opportunity to discover the truth that will reconcile the paradox. This, in turn, frees us from our fear. The ethic to discover our truth, the real truth, will rid ourselves of the false beliefs that belong to a relative, friend, teacher, religion, ideology, or culture.

So how did my fire walk go? I stood by and watched all my classmates walk on the coals slowly, methodically, and with great courage. In awe, I watched them go one by one. As I stood ready to go, I began to feel faint. I wanted to run. I wanted to be anywhere but there. I began to cry and shake. I thought that they were all stronger and braver than I was.

One of my fellow firewalkers walked up to me; he had been at the other end of the ten-foot rebar when we

[1]Messing, Richard, The Change Agent: on chronic human problems, freedom and ethics, a Kotel Business Community program.

walked together in unison to bend it with our throats. I trusted him implicitly. He was also crazy enough to do somersaults across one of our practice fire beds during the week.

I still hear his words in my head today. He asked me how much fire I had already walked during the week. I thought about it and responded, "Well, we walked at least seven to ten feet of red-hot coals for six consecutive nights."

He looked me straight in the eyes and said, "You have already walked forty feet this week. This walk should be a piece of cake. Now go!"

Off I went! It felt surreal. I was floating above the coals and never felt them. When I reached the other side, I saw a bell that signified the completion of training. I walked to the bell, rang it, turned around, and there were my classmates clapping and cheering. I stood there and took it all in for what seemed like an eternity.

Something inside me had changed... I realized that I had just accepted myself. I realized that if I could face my fears all week by walking broken glass, breaking arrows and rebar with my throat, and now walk over forty feet of fire, I could do anything I set my mind to.

I drove home that night in flip-flops with the air conditioner blowing on my feet. Even though I didn't burn my feet, remnants of the heat remained. As I drove home, I thought about what I had just accomplished and how I needed to make some major changes in my life. The next morning, I had the courage to start a conversation with my ex-husband about our relationship.

Six months later, I found myself driving to the state of Vermont with the car filled with my belongings. Vermont was always my special place, and I always wondered if I would enjoy it as much full-time as I did going up for vacations and long weekends.

At the age of fifty-four, I took the plunge and moved to a place where I didn't know anyone, started my business over, and began a new life. It's funny because my greatest fear has always been to be alone, yet I now live on the side of a mountain in a log home, and I can go weeks without seeing a traffic light. I have never felt more at peace. Work doesn't feel like work, and I feel joy when looking out over the mountain tops. I feel free.

Walking forty feet of red hot coals

Walking broken glass

Bending a straight ten foot piece of rebar from our throats by walking towards each other.

Exercise

Everyone goes through major changes in their life—their own fire walk. I invite you to reflect on your story and write about how you overcame your fear, identified your Lies, and discovered your Truth.

As you go through this book, you might want to keep a journal. I will also provide a link to videos that include tools and guided meditations to help you through some difficult times. These are not required in order to read this book, but they will deepen and enrich your experience.

Chapter Two

How the Lie Is Built

We all come from different backgrounds and different belief systems. We all believe that our beliefs are true. How is it possible that everyone's beliefs are true? Everyone has their belief, but within their belief, how do you know what is their Truth or the ultimate Truth?

For example, if you watch MSNBC, you believe what you are told is true. If someone else watches Fox News, and they believe what they are told is true. Which is it? Each person believes what they know is true; otherwise, they wouldn't believe it. It is a classic paradox, and according to the Merriam-Webster Dictionary, a paradox is a statement that is seemingly contradictory or opposed to common sense and yet is perhaps true. Our beliefs color the Truth. In every belief, there is a Truth and a Lie, or the Truth is missing.

In order to discover your truth, you need to connect with your map of the world. Your map of the world is your programming. It's how you see the world. How does your world get formed?

Here is a list of possibilities that formed your programming.

Gender	Family beliefs	Wealthy
Rural	Nerd	Middle Class
Urban	Smart	Poor
East Coast	Popular	Top Student
West Coast	Skin Color	Extravert
Country	Hair Color	introvert
South	Culture	Alcohol/Drugs
North	Trauma	Strict Family
Spiritual	Black sheep	Permissive Family
Catholic	Skinny	Video Games
Christian	Overweight	Violent Movies
Evangelical	Conservative	Attractive
Jewish	Free Spirit	Unattractive
Buddhist	Atheist	Outcast
Hindu	Public School	Popular
Muslim	Private School	Bullied
Christian Scientists	Boarding School	Athlete

Draw a circle on a piece of paper, pick a few items from the list that may have influenced your programming, and put them in the circle.

For example, Urban, Wealthy, Private School, Popular, and Extrovert

Draw a second circle and pick five items from the list that may represent the lens of a close friend or loved one, and write those items in the other circle.

For example, Rural, Poverty, Public School, Abused, Attractive, and Introvert

Imagine that each of those circles is a lens. If you place these lenses side by side, do you think they both portray the world exactly the same? Humans are far more complex and have many more items in our circles.

To add more complexity, most of what is in our circles—that which creates our lenses—resides in our unconscious. Are you aware that we don't have conscious access to most of our beliefs? They show up as triggers such as anger, jealousy, judgment, scarcity, and codependency, to name a few.

I invite you to create your lens and then ask at least three close friends or family members to come up with their circle and lens of how they see you. Are their answers consistent with each other? Is their vision of you consistent with your view of yourself?

I once facilitated this exercise for a group, and someone asked the group members to show what their lenses looked like. Everyone in the group had drawn a different picture! Some looked like binoculars, one looked like a monocular, and one looked like a magnifying glass. Not only was the information inside the lens unique to each person, but the actual portrayal of each lens was different!

We cannot see ourselves objectively. How often are you shocked to hear what other people see in you? The shock often happens because you didn't know that you had those traits or because you thought you were hiding them and couldn't believe that others could see them in you.

Some people are really good at hiding themselves, almost becoming invisible. Have you ever been at a party or an event and never noticed that someone was there the entire time? Some people are the opposite. They enter a space, and their energy takes up the entire room. All eyes are on them, they are charismatic, and everyone is drawn to them. We have all experienced both of those people.

What causes individuals to be invisible or seen? Your thoughts and the energy you put into that thought. *You are that powerful!* You can choose to make yourself larger than life, or you can choose to make yourself practically invisible. You have the choice every time you open your mouth or enter a room to decide who you plan to be at that moment.

People don't often realize that they can choose their emotions. You get to choose how you react to experiences; you may choose joy, pain, fear, or fearlessness. Your emotions are a direct reflection of your inner beliefs.

We are all members of a tribe. When I say tribe, I mean your family or a group with beliefs in common such as people with the same culture, religion, and beliefs. What happens when you feel like you don't fit in? I have a friend who said she never felt like she fit into her family. Her family doesn't share the same beliefs.

We joked about the 1960s television show, *The Munsters*, where the dad, Herman, looks like Frankenstein; the wife, Lily, and her father are vampires, and Lily and Herman's son Eddie is a werewolf. The niece, Marilyn, is "normal," blonde-haired, blue-eyed, and feels like an outcast. We called my friend Marilyn. Just because you don't fit in doesn't mean you are wrong or broken. Though when you feel outnumbered, it can be painful to hold different beliefs.

Many people will get kicked out of their tribes—families, religious groups, social groups—for having beliefs outside the norm. If you are not fully comfortable with who you are, someone with different beliefs can make you feel uncomfortable.

Often when a person gets triggered by someone or something, it is because something remains unhealed inside of the person who is triggered, something they don't like about themselves. Once that trigger is healed, the reaction fades away. When the triggering event no longer sparks a reaction, the unconscious wound is healed.

I used to get triggered when people questioned me about my beliefs or my course of study, especially when they called me "weird." It used to hurt, and I felt like an outcast. However, once I owned that weird part of me, saw it as my gift, and truly embraced it, I was no longer triggered by being called weird. I actually love and embrace the weird part of me now. It's what has made me unique and special.

We all have those parts of us that get triggered. When you get triggered, stop and go inward. Ask yourself why you are getting so upset. The answer may surprise you; it may be a part of you that is unhealed. Bringing it up to your awareness is the first step to healing it.

Depending on the culture, it can be dangerous to have different beliefs than your tribe. Your survival may depend on the tribe, especially if the family has strict beliefs and rules or is deeply religious.

People may also become angry at you for speaking your truth. That could be because they may be living a lie, and they can't handle someone stepping out of the tribe. They didn't dare to step out, so they may resent you for your courage and take it out on you.

So many things influence who we are. How do we know what belongs to us and what belongs to others? Whose beliefs are we walking around with? Our grandmother's? Our first-grade teachers? The bully on the school bus? Our religious leader? Our best friend? The New York Times?

Few of us realize the influence our beliefs have on us. We often don't recognize that our beliefs can skew our entire worldview. Most of us don't realize that we are even ignorant, or as Richard Messing puts it, "we are ignorant of being ignorant."

Even the word ignorant triggers people because the word is often equated with being stupid. According to the Merriam-Webster Dictionary, ignorance is defined as lacking knowledge or information. *We all lack information when we make judgments and decisions about others and situations.*

According to Nassim Taleb, "The problem with experts is that they do not know what they do not know," and Richard Messing also likes to say, "Just because something makes sense doesn't make it true. Just because something doesn't make sense doesn't mean it isn't true."

When we see things from different perspectives, what we see looks different. An example of this is the story of the blind men and the elephant.

THE ELEPHANT AND THE BLIND MEN

Once there were six blind men who lived in a village. One day another villager exclaimed, "Hey, there is an elephant in the village today."

The blind men had no idea what an elephant was, so they decided that even though they would not be able to see it, they would go and touch it and experience what an elephant is anyway. Every one of them touched the elephant.

The first man said, "The elephant is like a pillar," after he touched his leg.

"It's like a rope," said the second man after he touched the tail.

After touching the trunk, the third man said, "You are mistaken; it is like a thick branch of a tree."

After touching the ear of the elephant, the fourth man said, "The three of you are wrong. It's like a big hand fan."

The fifth man told everyone that he had the answer. After he touched the belly of the elephant, he exclaimed, "It's a huge wall!"

The sixth man, after touching the elephant's tusk, said. "You're all wrong. It is like a solid pipe."

They argued and argued about the elephant, each one insisting that he was right. A wise man was passing by and saw them arguing. He asked them what they were arguing over, and they responded that they could not agree on what an elephant looks like. The wise man gently explained to them that they were all right. "Each one of you has touched the elephant in a different place. The elephant has all those features each of you claim."

The six blind men were relieved. After realizing each of them was right in his own observation, they stopped arguing.

How often have you made decisions about someone and judged someone and found out later you were completely wrong because you only had part of the truth? What was your lens?

To discover your lens, consider what has influenced your life. An important factor is where you were born. What is your perspective about people who live in other parts of the country—north, south, east, west, rural, or urban?

I once worked in New York City on Fashion Avenue in the garment center. One day I was talking with a co-worker who was from the south, and she had a strong southern accent. She told me that she was taking elocution lessons so that she could learn to speak like a New Yowka. I laughed as I listened to her imitation of a thick New York accent. She felt that her southern accent prevented people in New York City from taking her seriously. Incredibly, some perceptions are formed purely based on an accent.

What was your home life like? Did you have emotional support, were you left to fend for yourself, were you abused, were you deeply loved? People project beliefs developed in childhood into situations throughout their lives. If you were abandoned, you might believe that all people abandon you. If you believe that all people will abandon you, you will keep attracting people who abandon you, and you will prove to yourself repeatedly that people abandon you until you heal it.

We all have something called a reticular activating system that filters information. It will find what you are looking for unconsciously, filter that information, and bring it to your conscious awareness. For example, have you ever noticed when you buy a brand-new car, you see that model everywhere? When I buy a new car, I like to think I am buying something unique and different. I might choose a special model or color—something that reflects my unique personality. I can't tell you how frustrated I get after I buy a new car and I start to see that model car everywhere. I wanted a unique car, one that would stand out, and now they appear to be everywhere. It wasn't that more of those cars were on the road. Rather my reticular activating system filtered what I was seeing.

The reticular activating system works the same way with our beliefs. If you were abandoned as a child and subsequently believe people will abandon you or that people are untrustworthy, you will start attracting people and situations that match your belief. You will repeatedly attract people who abandon you, or you can't trust, reinforcing that belief, and therefore you are now convinced that people abandon you or you can't trust people. You create these situations unconsciously. The first step is awareness of these behaviors in order to heal them. Take responsibility for your actions, forgive, and heal the pain from that event.

When you forgive, heal, and become neutral about a situation or belief, you will no longer attract circumstances that reflect that belief. That's how you know that the belief is healed. Of course, we all have degrees and layers of issues. Something might not completely go away because there is another aspect of it left that you haven't dealt with, or you may be tested for a while to make sure it's gone.

Was education pushed at home? Were you pushed to excel at school? Did your parents take an interest in your education? Some cultures believe in education, and everything is about grades and getting into the perfect college. Some cultures are about going to work early to help the family financially.

How important were sports? Were athletic activities fun and casual, or were you an athlete who participated on elite travel teams? Did you enjoy it? Were you pushed in sports to earn a scholarship, or was the sports scholarship your idea?

There is a Lie that parents need to live vicariously through their children in sports. I love sports, and both of my children are athletes. My daughter was a lacrosse goalie in high school, and her team won the New

Hampshire State Championship. People used to ask me what I thought was the most difficult position on the lacrosse team. I always answered, "Mother of the goalie!"

I have consistently observed inappropriate behavior of parents on the sidelines of youth and high school sports. I watched countless parents live out their unfulfilled dreams via their children by screaming at the child, the coaches, and the referees. I even watched parents get banned from games! The Lie they told themselves was that these children were a direct reflection and extension of themselves, or they needed to get a scholarship in order to cover the cost of college.

When my son was in middle school, he wanted to play football. I was not thrilled with the idea, but I knew how important it was to him. One day at practice, I was standing on the sidelines, and I noticed a group of kids standing in a circle. They were throwing grass and kicking someone. I took note of the jersey numbers, and before I reached the circle, an ambulance showed up. One boy was on the ground writhing around in pain, holding his knee.

While he was in the ambulance being taken to the hospital, I ran over to one of the coaches and told him I had the numbers of the kids who did this. He looked at me and told me I was just a mom, and I didn't know what I saw. I was shocked.

I investigated and discovered that all of the boys involved in that incident were the coaches' sons and star players. They were supposed to be heading to the league "super bowl" the next weekend, and the coaches were not going to jeopardize their opportunity to win. Their team was undefeated and unscored upon. Not one of the coaches or board members would talk to me about what I witnessed; they just continued to dismiss me.

Out of frustration, I wrote an editorial in the local paper about what happened, and that night, the president of the local football league called me and told me that he knew where I lived and he was going to come after me. This was middle-school football!

I grabbed my children, shut the lights off in my house, and went to the police department to report the incident and the phone call. I spoke to my son's coach, told him what happened, and he sent someone over to the home of the league president to tell him to back off.

I got together with a number of parents who were just as upset as I was, and we decided to start a competing Pop Warner football program. Within nine months, we had one hundred and twenty kids, brand new jerseys, coaches, raised money for equipment, and we were ready to go!

What compelled these coaches and their organizations to be so obsessed with winning in sports that they were willing to compromise the health and safety of players? What were they teaching these children? What happened to teaching children good sportsmanship?

Awareness of Your Lies

What happened to a good healthy debate in politics? Where do your political beliefs come from? Are you conservative, liberal, or somewhere in between? Do you tend to vote and think along party lines? Why? Is it because that is how your family voted, and those values were passed on to you? Did you give another party a chance, or is your perception about the other party so skewed that you only see it through a lens of negativity?

Did you grow up with money? What did your parents say about people with money? If you had money growing up, did you have to work, and were you taught to appreciate money and have a relationship with it? Were you given what you needed and didn't have to work so you could focus on other things such as sports or school work?

What motivates you at work? Money, appreciation, being of service to others, understanding others better, educating others, or being a visionary and inventing something new?

Knowing these things about yourself helps you better identify your beliefs and bring them into your conscious mind from your subconscious. Be curious. There is no right or wrong. This process is about discovering which beliefs resonate with you. Question why you have your beliefs. What is your motivation to believe in them?

The Importance of Boundaries

I have different types of boundaries in my relationships. I have people in my life who carry very different beliefs than I do. I honor and respect that they see the world through their lenses. If I oppose someone else's views, it's not my responsibility to change their mind. I wouldn't like it if someone tried to push their views on me.

It's important to maintain dialogue and be curious. Ask questions and find out why someone believes what they believe. You may learn something. Or you may teach them something. We learn through trust. When you create a bond of trust, people will be more open to listening. That is why you must keep in mind that they view the world through their lens.

Are we arrogant enough to believe we know everything? I have found that the older I get, the less I know about everything. I have let go of many beliefs in my life that I once thought were true that no longer have any relevance to me whatsoever. When you dig in your heels and refuse to listen to what someone has to say, you miss out on an opportunity to learn more about that person, and you miss an opportunity to learn more about yourself.

If someone else's opinion triggers you, what stops you from hearing what they have to say? Understanding is a way to peace. Acknowledging what someone has to say is important. We all want to experience being seen and heard. Even if you don't like what someone has to say, honor that it's important to them. When you only surround yourself with people who think and sound like you, you miss out on a learning opportunity.

I have a group of friends who are my trusted advisors. They are the ones who share my core values, and we have much in common. I feel safe in that group—free and not judged. As much as I love my tribe of trusted advisors, it's essential to engage with groups with various beliefs. Maintain an open mind, exchange different ideas, allow yourself to be flexible, and maybe even change your opinion when new information comes in. Evaluate your beliefs often, and don't forget that we are all ignorant of being ignorant.

As you can see, the Lie is built in many ways. We don't get the option as a baby to say whether we want something in our life or not. Our programming just becomes part of our everyday normal life. We live it and think it's normal and don't think of a reason to change it. A few exceptional rebels decide that traditional family programming isn't for them, but sometimes the programming encourages rebellion. You don't know if the rebellious belief is really yours; you just know that the original Lie is not for you. It takes a lot of courage to recognize the Lies and be willing to change the Lie to your Truth. How do you even know what your Truth is?

Exercise

Make a list of people who trigger you. Take each person in that list and write a list of why they trigger you. Get specific, don't write, "Because they are stupid."

- Go inward, ask yourself why you dislike this person so much.
- Who do they remind you of?
- What do they represent to you?
- Is it possible to have compassion for them and understand that they are doing the best they can with what they have?
- They see the world through different eyes. Their lens is different from yours. Get curious.
- If you forgive them and let go of what triggers you, how will your life change?

Your mind automatically wants to keep you safe. It will do everything possible to ensure your survival. We often react, and we don't even know why. This is an opportunity to look at the specifics and break them down. Often I find that when I get triggered, it's an unresolved wound inside of me that I am projecting onto the other person. When I heal that wound, I am no longer triggered by that person. My goal is always to reach a state of neutrality. When I'm neutral, I don't react; I just observe. Maybe there is a lesson in this for me? What lessons and gifts will you receive from the people who trigger you?

Chapter Three

The Lie That You Are Not Smart

Dr. Bruce Lipton suggests that our programming is founded on our first seven years and that ninety-five percent of our life's results come from that subconscious programming.

How often have you heard yourself repeat things that were said to you as a child? Things you swore you would never say to your own children.

- *If you keep making that face, it's going to freeze like that!*
- *Because I said so, that's why!*
- *Waste not, want not.*
- *Finish everything on your plate; there are children starving in Africa.*
- *Money doesn't grow on trees.*
- *Stop crying, or I'll give you something to cry about!*

Writing these phrases brought me right back to my childhood. So many of our beliefs stem from the people, places, and experiences we've had in our early lives. We are here to create and express ourselves. Yet, unfortunately, many schools and work environments suppress creativity and self-expression.

Over the years, I've seen a theme in my clients, a common belief. They believe they are not smart. I, too, have carried this belief. I was not a great student, and I grew up thinking that I was stupid.

When you think about it, most schools teach linguistic and math intelligence, yet according to Dr. Howard Gardener, nine types of intelligence are available to us. That leaves seven kinds of intelligence unexplored during the formative school-age years. No wonder so many people believe they're not smart. I wonder how different I would have felt about myself if I knew early on what I was really good at and was taught to focus and excel in that area? Some people are lucky enough to figure out their innate intelligence types early. But that is a rare few.

So many of us judge ourselves, our children, and others on high school grades, standardized tests, and the college attended, if any. Yet many very successful people had poor grades and didn't go to college. Their success may be due to high emotional intelligence, drive, or athletic or artistic talent. We don't all fit in a nice box where everyone thinks and behaves the same. Getting straight A's may be important for some things and not for others. I would definitely want my surgeon to have graduated near or at the top of her class!

According to an article, "Gardner's Multiple Theory of Intelligences," by Kendra Cherry,[2] Gardner's theory eventually became controversial because both psychologists and educators argue that his definition of intelligence is too broad and that his intelligences simply represent talents, personality traits, and abilities. For me, however, his concept changed my life. It helped me realize that my gift is not memorizing information for tests. My gift is intrapersonal intelligence. When I realized that, it helped me understand that I had a unique gift and a unique way of learning. Maybe you will recognize your intelligence in the list below.

Visual and Spatial Intelligence: These people are good at visualizing things. They are great with directions. They make great architects and artists. They recognize patterns. Sailors look at the water to see the patterns the

---

[2] https://www.verywellmind.com/gardners-theory-of-multiple-intelligences-2795161

wind makes on the water to see the best and fastest way to move forward.

*Linguistic-Verbal Intelligence*L: These people are great writers, speakers, and communicators. They love reading and writing and may make good teachers, professional speakers, and journalists.

Logical-Mathematical Intelligence: These people are really good at problem-solving. They see patterns and think logically. These people make great engineers, mathematicians, scientists, and accountants.

Bodily-Kinesthetic Intelligence: These people are amazing at body control. They are often dancers, athletes, and coaches. They like doing things with their hands and are often excellent builders and sculptors.

Musical Intelligence: These people think in rhythm, patterns, and sounds. They excel at playing and creating music. They can sing, play instruments, and write and produce music.

Interpersonal Intelligence: These people understand nonverbal communication. They can intuit people's motivations. A salesperson has great interpersonal intelligence, as do psychologists, social workers, and politicians.

Intrapersonal Intelligence: These people have high emotional intelligence. They are empathic, good at being self-aware and analyzing ideas, exploring relationships with others, and assessing personal strengths. These people are philosophers, religious leaders, and theorists.

Naturalistic Intelligence: These people are interested in botany and biology. They feel connected to nature. They could be farmers, florists, forest rangers, and biologists.

Existential Intelligence: These people can handle deep questions such as the meaning of existence. It's one of the most complex of the nine types of intelligence listed in Gardner's research. They are philosophers, clergy, or deeply spiritual people looking for the meaning of life or what happens after death.

The Lie that We All Think the Same

My son Max was in elementary school, and one day he came home with a painting of a lighthouse. I loved it so much that I had it framed. I saw in the local paper a listing for an upcoming children's art exhibit, and I entered his lighthouse into the show. I remember walking in and seeing ten identical light houses. I was shocked. They were all well done, something for each of the children to be proud of, but my personal training in art was about each person creating their own interpretation of what they saw.

I remember thinking it was a metaphor for how we are taught in life. We are taught to be like others and fit into a box. The Lie we often tell ourselves is that we will be successful and happy if we do the right things. I have seen many people who graduated high school with good grades, went to a good college, got a high-paying job, became unhappy, and felt trapped. They had done all of the "right" things according to society's guidelines for happiness, and yet they would come home from work and medicate themselves for depression or engage in some sort of addictive behavior to numb their feelings.

Dream and You Will Find Your Truth

People who think outside the box will often quit their jobs, take a risk to start a new business, go into the peace corps, sail around the world, backpack across Europe, or live in a tiny home off the grid. Yet they hear messages that they are bad or something is wrong with them. They are often implored to be "normal." Normal is considered safe to many. When people talk to others of their dreams, others will project their fears and their unfulfilled dreams onto the dreamer because they are too afraid to take a risk of their own.

Changemakers influence the world. They are incredible dreamers who are passionate about their cause. They are willing to risk everything for what they believe in. Where would our world be without them? We would live in a world with no progress.

How do you overcome the negative influence of others? First, dream, then, you must believe in yourself and your cause, strategize, visualize, and take action. None of this works unless you take action. Too many ideas die a sad, slow death because people didn't believe in themselves, got talked out of a creative idea, or couldn't find the courage to leave their current situation.

You must be flexible. You must be willing to try different ways to get what you want.

What lies do you believe about money, how smart you are, if you are worthy of love, or if you even have something worth saying or doing? We all have something worth saying or doing. We are all a unique thumbprint. We are all here for a reason and a purpose. We actually need purpose in order to be happy.

What does being smart even mean? Who created that standard? If someone is an amazing artist but fails a math test, does that mean he isn't smart? We allow others to create standards for us, allow ourselves to be judged, and if we don't meet their standards, we must not be smart.

With age, I now recognize that I am smart, although it may not be the kind of smart that aces high school exams. I have a unique way of accomplishing what I need to accomplish. I am gifted at connecting people to one another. It's like I have a database of people in my brain, and whenever I hear about someone looking for someone with a particular skill or shared value, I immediately connect them. I could do that all day long; it brings me such joy. No one taught me this skill; it is simply a part of me being me. Could other people be connectors? Absolutely, but they will do it a different way than I do it. There is no wrong way. We all have a unique thumbprint that we are here to offer the world.

I spoke with a friend recently who has had many people ask her to teach them how to connect with their inner wisdom. She thought it would be fun to introduce this concept and share this knowledge with people via weekend retreats. The problem was that she didn't know how to teach what she does—her process. It was holding her back. I suggested that she teach people how to find their inner wisdom themselves. Just guide them towards the outcome and set the intention. She couldn't teach people to connect with their inner wisdom in her exact style, yet they could find their own way with her guidance.

Have you ever gotten a recipe from someone, and even though you follow it exactly, it doesn't come out the same? Each person has a unique way of accomplishing a goal. The best way to show people their Truth is for them to set their intention and let them discover their gifts to reach their goal. When you Lie to yourself by saying you are not smart, you waste potential. The more you release the Lies, the easier it will be to find out how smart you are because there will be nothing in the way to keep you from thinking otherwise.

Exercise

In your journal, write the answer to these questions down. Close your eyes when you answer these questions, and note if there is a sensation in your body. How does it feel to revisit your old goals and dreams? Is there a longing?

If so, what do you want to do about it?

- Do you have a dream or a goal you allowed yourself to be talked out of?
- Did someone instill fear into you, so you walked away?
- Make a list of those dreams and goals and write down the fears associated with each of them.
- Do you still feel connected to any of them?
- If you eliminated your fear and someone could guarantee that it would be successful, would you still do it?

Chapter Four

Lies We Tell Ourselves

Most of us believe that life has to be hard. Hard work pays off. Everything has to be hard, or it's not worth doing. Yes, hard work does pay off, but have you ever thought about times when everything felt easy and effortless? Do you know what it feels like to be in the zone? What were you doing at the time—in those moments when time feels like it is flying, you are having fun, and it doesn't feel like work? That's when you are being you! When I work with a client, speak on a stage, or give a workshop, I feel joy. Time flies quickly, and what I'm doing doesn't feel like work.

I didn't always understand my gifts and what to do with them. I spent many years confused, believing that I didn't have anything to offer. When I began my journey of studying the subconscious mind, I became obsessed. I couldn't stop studying. I read hundreds of books; I was constantly looking for teachers. I was so hungry for knowledge; it felt like I had been starving my entire life.

Once I accumulated enough knowledge, I decided that I wanted to go out and speak professionally. When I decided I would start speaking in public, I was terrified. I didn't believe I had anything unique to say, but I felt compelled to do it. To help me hone my skills, a friend recommended that I explore Toastmasters, an organization that teaches public speaking and leadership skills. I found a Toastmasters club when I lived in Concord, New Hampshire, and I fell in love with the people in that group. They encouraged me, supported me, and challenged me to be the best speaker I could possibly be.

I still remember my first couple of speeches. I would practice over and over again for hours, standing in front of the mirror, watching my movements, making sure I looked natural and fluid. Then, when I stood in front of the group, everything began to flow. I started to feel more and more relaxed and actually began enjoying myself in front of the room.

One of my mentors, Steve Gamlin, would inspire me and encourage me to use humor on the stage. Not only is he an amazing speaker, but he was also a former professional radio DJ with his own morning show, and he was a standup comedian.

One day, I was running late for a Toastmasters meeting and walked in while Steve was in the middle of an extemporaneous speech. He was so quick on his feet that he included me in his talk. I walked through the door, and as if I was walking in on cue as part of his speech, he put his arm around me and added me into his story. His timing was impeccable. We had a great laugh after that. He encouraged me to start speaking at different organizations such as Rotary, Lions, corporate lunch and learns, and networking groups. Finally, I got my first big speaking gig, The Depression and Bi-Polar Association of Boston, Massachusetts, at McLean Hospital Boston.

Steve offered to help me prepare. It was my first big speech, and the audience would be over one hundred people! He helped me sprinkle my talk with humor, and I practiced it repeatedly. I hired a videographer so I could use snippets of my talk on social media. I was so excited! I remember getting on stage in front of everyone. I began my talk with a one-liner Steve helped me craft, and all I heard were crickets. I began to sweat and speed up my talk. I imagined an old-fashioned hook coming from the side of the stage and pulling me off.

Then, I began to breathe and remind myself that I was a professional. I continued my forty-five-minute talk and was met with complete silence. The only one laughing at my jokes was me. Then, as soon as I completed my presentation, something remarkable happened. The entire room lit up. Hands went up everywhere!

I was so confused. I answered questions for twenty minutes until the facilitators decided to wrap things up. They allowed one last question or comment, and I will never forget that comment as long as I live. When the audience member spoke, she said that when you are on lithium, you can't feel the high highs or the low lows; you are just numb all of the time.

When I signed up to speak, I thought I was speaking to therapists and psychiatrists. At the moment of that comment, I realized that I wasn't speaking to a room full of professionals. I was speaking to a room full of heavily medicated depressed and bipolar people.

Lesson 1: When applying to speak, always ask who your audience is.

Lesson 2: Always maintain professionalism no matter what.

Lesson 3: There is always a lesson, be grateful.

I tell this story to illustrate the disadvantage of making assumptions. I was seeing the world through my lens.

A part of me was ready to walk away from speaking that day. Another part of me couldn't wait to get in front of another audience. The biggest lesson I learned from that experience was nothing ever seems like it appears. The Lie I told myself was that I was terrible, and the audience hated me. That was the farthest thing from the truth; they loved me. I even got a client out of it.

I had to stand in my Truth and be me. I had to override the voice in my head telling me to run, to give up, to just walk off the stage. We all have adversity in our lives and beliefs that will sabotage us, but we need to become sovereign. It is imperative to stand up for ourselves, believe in ourselves, and know who we are at the core.

I recently watched a movie about Lucille Ball. She always made her comedy look easy and effortless. I discovered that she was not naturally funny in real life. She rehearsed over and over and made it look easy. Her gift was her physical comedy, drive, and creativity.

Have you ever seen a beautiful woman start to point out all the things that make her ugly; meanwhile, you stood there wishing you had a fraction of her beauty? Perhaps she made up Lies about her legs—her legs are too long, too short, too muscular, not muscular enough. Her hair is curly, and she wishes it was straight.

It's painful to watch other people go through this process. If it's not okay for others to do this, why is it okay for you?

We cannot be happy while we believe the lies that we tell ourselves. What are your lies?

The Lie We Tell Ourselves in Relationships

According to Jordan Peterson, a Canadian Clinical Psychologist, if you betray me, I may have to adjust my actions and my perceptions of you, but I may also have to adjust my perception of myself. I may start to doubt how I am in relationships.

If I am gullible enough to fall for that, what will I have to do to change how I am in other relationships? How do I prevent this from ever happening again?

What happens when we change how we are in a relationship based on something someone else did or said to us? The Lie you just told yourself is that something was wrong with you, and, therefore, you can never be like that in a relationship again.

It could be a lesson you need to learn. Is this really a pattern in your life, or do you happen to be dating the wrong guy, and someone else who is better for you is waiting to come into your life?

What if this betrayal had nothing to do with you and the other person did something out of character, was triggered, or misbehaved for some other random reason, and you changed your beliefs and behaviors based on that Lie. You have now created a disaster in your life. You have now changed a belief, which will activate your reticular activating system, and that part of your brain will begin to attract people and circumstances that reflect betrayal, proving to you over and over again that people cannot be trusted in relationships.

This is how Lies become our Truth. An example of this is someone who cheats on you. You suddenly think that this is your fault; you also decide that men in relationships cannot be trusted. Now you have just created a Lie through which you will view the world. You changed your belief to accommodate a Lie, you now change your behavior based on a Lie, and thus you will attract men who cheat in order to confirm that Lie.

> *"Three things cannot be hidden; the sun, the moon, and a lie."* Buddha

1: Be your own truth seeker.

2: Go inward and discern what is true and what is not.

3: What is true for some people is not true for others.

Relationships are tricky because we act out our unhealed traumas and wounds. We actually have something called a wound-mate. Wound-mate relationships can be compelling. They feel like love, but they are not love. The relationship becomes about healing our unmet needs through the relationship, not from the root cause where it started. We never want someone to complete us.

In the movie *Jerry Maguire there is a* famous scene where Tom Cruise says to Renée Zellweger, "You complete me!" If someone says that to you, *run*—do not walk—from this relationship! This mindset is a recipe for disaster. If someone is not whole, doesn't feel good about who they are, and doesn't love themselves, how will they love you? The best thing to do is to do the work, go back to the root cause and heal that.

What if you don't know what the root cause is? The best part about working with the subconscious mind is that you don't have to! Your subconscious mind knows, and it does all of the work. When you communicate with your subconscious mind, you just have to ask it to take you to the memory of the initial event where the Lie became programmed. Once you are in that memory, you can shift the way you feel about that event, thus changing the way you perceive it. You can't change what happened, but you do have the ability to change the way you feel about it.

Exercise

Imagine a five year old version of yourself in front of you. Then recall some of the negative comments you have said to yourself in the current day.

Now imagine saying those very things to your 5 year old self.

- Why is it okay to say mean and inappropriate Lies to your older self but not to your younger self?
- What's different?
- You create with your words, what do you want to create in your life?
- Always remember, we are all doing the best we can with what we have.

Chapter Five

The Lie Created by the Dark Side of Your Emotional Needs

Your subconscious always tries to make you feel safe. The job of your subconscious mind is to consistently check what is going on and grab onto answers that make the most sense. I invite you to ask yourself, what are some beliefs that make you feel safe?

Many people feel safe in the belief that food is love. Food can be comforting, but it is a temporary fix. The Lie we tell ourselves is that we will feel better after that pint of Ben and Jerry's ice cream, that piece of chocolate cake, or that second or third helping of lasagna.

When you think about the emotion of anger, you get angry. Anger does not happen to you. Why do some people rage over a simple thing, and others have a really long fuse? Some people choose not to deal with their anger at all. The point I am making is that your emotions are a choice. Emotions are healthy, and it's important to feel them, process them and then use them as fuel to accomplish something or let them go.

Unprocessed emotions can make you feel unsafe. They show up in all kinds of ways. They show up as nightmares, anxiety, phobias, depression, and grief. Unprocessed emotions can cause triggers. We carry triggers that bring up negative emotions that make us feel unsafe. Smells, sounds, phrases, people, places, and things can all be anchors. Anchors are words, smells, sounds, or touches that remind you of other events and happenings. What song transports you to a memory?

Smells and sounds are excellent at prompting memories. The smell of pine or the sound of sleigh bells may remind you of Christmas. An anchor may take you to a memory, a snapshot of your life through the lens that you saw it from in a time gone by. That memory is from the perspective you experienced it, at the age it happened.

As you know, your six-year-old self experiences something differently than your adult self. You can hear a story from someone who lived through the very same circumstance as you, and they will remember it entirely differently. When you travel back to a childhood memory, see it through your adult perspective, heal it, and forgive the other people, the situation, and even yourself. The way you see the world changes. Over time your lens will completely change, and you get a new one.

An example of this Lie is if you have experienced abandonment by a parent. You see the world through the lens that people who are important to you abandon you, and you will attract people and circumstances that will confirm your belief over and over again, proving that people abandon you. Therefore it's not safe to be intimate and have close relationships even though you long for connection. Your unconscious mind always searches for situations and circumstances that match your beliefs. Unconscious beliefs create the largest portion of our lens. When you change your lens, the Lie no longer is in charge, and you are in control and can change the way you experience the world.

We carry emotions in our physical bodies. When we suppress our emotions, they have to go somewhere. They can manifest in our lives in all kinds of physical and mental issues if not addressed and healed.

Throughout my journey working with people, one of the things I found to be pervasive is the need to constantly fill that empty space inside of ourselves with something.

Most people think of addiction as drugs, alcohol, food, sex, and gambling. Addiction can go much further than that. We use addictions to keep us from achieving our goals and excuses for not fully actualizing our dreams. We can be addicted to being a victim, being angry, working, perfection, shopping, working out, chocolate, smart phones, caffeine, sugar, plastic surgery, tanning, love, drama, fear, grief, pain, and illness. These are just the tip of the iceberg.

Addictions can be anything that keeps us from being fully present and sovereign. What do I mean by that? We all have a saboteur. A part of us that keeps us from getting what we really want. That part created a Lie to protect us. Often it's a younger part of ourselves that is unhealed from a childhood wound. This part thinks it's doing a really good job protecting you, but it's actually Lying to you.

Think about someone who uses perfection as a way to sabotage themselves. No matter how smart they are or how hard they work, they will never be good enough. Perfectionism is actually a form of procrastination. You will keep working on something and working on it, and the Lie is that no matter how much you work on whatever it is, it will never be good enough. You will beat yourself up repeatedly, proving yourself right because you didn't accomplish the goal.

Many people understand the impact of addiction on their emotions, but most people don't fully realize the impact of sarcasm and how it affects yourself and others.

I have found that addiction and sarcasm block intimacy and don't allow you to experience love fully. Depending on where you live, sarcasm will either be a big part of your life, or you won't understand it at all. The northeastern part of the United States is filled with sarcasm, especially in the Boston area. The problem with sarcasm is that the subconscious mind doesn't know the difference between a real experience, a movie, or a joke. That's why we can have nightmares after a scary movie.

Everyone has had someone in their life who is sarcastic. These people love to tease and can be very well-meaning, but studies have shown that when people tease, they are often unaware that the person they are speaking to actually feels the comment at a deep level. Your subconscious will now create a Lie about yourself based upon a sarcastic comment someone said to you.

When someone is sarcastic all of the time, they are actually blocking connection. The other people in their lives put up an unconscious or conscious wall to prevent themselves from being hurt. The receiver of sarcasm will put up a barrier, but did you ever think about the possibility that the person who is giving out the barbs is doing it unconsciously to protect themselves from being hurt? Sarcasm can be used as a protection from anger, fear of getting hurt, social awkwardness, or insecurity, just to name a few.

Sarcastic remarks always carry a bit of truth. When someone is angry or jealous, instead of complimenting someone, they may send a little barb. The receiver instantly feels the jab and may experience hurt feelings. When we are not feeling good about ourselves, we sometimes use sarcasm to make us feel better because we're projecting our feelings onto others. The problem is that it isolates us and makes us feel lonely. Sarcastic people don't want to be alone, but on the other hand, they don't trust people, so they push them away. Most of this behavior is unconscious.

Imagine a police officer directing traffic. One hand gestures traffic to come towards them, and the other hand gestures traffic to stop. That's the message we send out with sarcasm. We stop people from coming close but at the same time long for intimacy and closeness.

Have you ever seen a child run, trip, and fall? Now imagine if while the child is on the ground, in shock, scanning their body to see if they are hurt, someone jokingly yells out, "Did you have a nice trip?" or "Have a nice fall?" Close your eyes and imagine being in that child's place. Do you feel joy and expansiveness, or does your body constrict? Now imagine someone coming up to that child and asking them if they are okay, assuring them that they are there for them in case they need some help. Close your eyes and imagine that scenario. Does that feel expansive and loving or restrictive in your body?

When exposed to sarcasm often, your subconscious feels it and experiences it as a criticism or attack. Your body will automatically constrict and feel isolated. The next time something happens to someone, or you are just joking around, be mindful of what you say. You might be hurting someone's feelings, or worse yet, you might be creating a Lie and influencing someone's belief system. Your words are that powerful!

Chapter Six

The Lie That Money Is the Root of All Evil

The topic of money is so loaded. I often talk to groups about money mindset. I have a PowerPoint slide that shows a mansion, and I ask people in the room to tell me about the people in that house. What is their family like? How do they live? Are they happy? The answers I usually get are that they hate each other, the parents are getting a divorce, the kids are all on drugs, and they can't afford to heat the house.

People will quote from the bible that the love of money is the root of all evil. How about the verse that states, "It is easier for a camel to go through the eye of a needle than a rich man to enter into the kingdom of heaven." That has been quoted to me many times. People tell me it's because rich people generally put their focus and trust in their material world instead of God.

That is a Lie. Are there people obsessed with making money and having nice things? Yes. Are many wealthy people philanthropists? Yes. Yet so many of us see wealthy people as unhappy, greedy, and materialistic. How can we make these gross generalizations? Look how the movie and television industry creates Lies by portraying people with money as greedy, miserable, and selfish.

There is a paradox in this situation. I see people with money and without money who are materialistic and people with and without money who are spiritual and give back to others and their communities. We all deserve happiness, success, and abundance, yet we are conditioned to believe we are not deserving of it or that we shouldn't want it. That is a huge Lie.

People have many different issues around money. For some, money comes easily and effortlessly. Some people inherit money. Some people don't believe they are worthy and deserving of money, and some people have scarcity issues from their childhood. The interesting thing about people with scarcity issues is that this perspective is not held solely by people without money. Some people have the ability to make a lot of money, but it never seems like enough; they can't seem to hold on to it.

The lens that you see money through is a lens that will often define your life. Did you know that seventy percent of people who win the lottery go bankrupt? It's because they don't have a relationship with money. A million dollars can sound like a lot of money, but taxes take a huge chunk out of the winnings. The next step is to maybe buy a house, exciting, right? Most don't consider the cost of maintaining the house and property taxes?

Money is an exchange of energy. You receive money in exchange for an act or service and how much you value that service. How often have you seen two people do the exact same thing for a living, and one person is wealthy while the other struggles financially.

When I worked for an innovative start-up company, we developed programs using a combination of guided meditation, virtual reality, and binaural beats to help people with concentration, memory retention, stress reduction, and so much more. I was excited about this company because I thought it would be an amazing opportunity to help thousands, if not millions of people.

One day, I had a meeting with someone high up in a human resource service company who was willing to put together a pilot program for us to see how their company members would like it. The executive requested that we send several headsets—which were used for part of the guided meditation system—so that someone who had never seen a virtual reality headset could open the box and have immediate access to the necessary tools.

The startup company owner complained to me that he had limited resources and didn't want to spend a couple of thousand dollars on new packaging and to send out headsets. The HR company had the potential to set us up with over 2,000 companies! The owner didn't want to invest in packaging that would create ease of use for the clients. Being an entrepreneur is not easy. Knowing how and when to allocate limited resources is a complicated process, but to me, this was a no-brainer. Last I heard, this potentially life-changing company was no longer in business.

What is the Lie you tell yourself about money and people who have money?

Exercise

What does money mean to you?

Write down the following:

Do you believe that money is abundant and flows to you, or do you believe that money is for others?

Where did that belief come from?

What was your parents' relationship with money?

What were you taught about money?

Are you happy with your belief?

What would happen if you were to change your belief around money?

How would that change your life?

Would you live your life differently?

Chapter Seven

The Lies You Inherit

Did you know that your great-great-grandmother may have an influence on your behavior and decision-making without you even knowing?

Not only do we carry with us beliefs from our childhood, but we also inherit beliefs from our parents, grandparents, and up to seven generations back! How do you know what belief is yours, what belongs to a relative who died long ago, or stems from childhood trauma? Every belief determines your perception, and every perception determines your behavior. Learn to discover the beliefs that are not yours and find your Truth.

According to the article, "Fearful Memories Passed Down to Mouse Descendants," found in *Scientific American* magazine, excerpted from *Nature Magazine*, Kerry Ressler, a neurobiologist and psychiatrist at Emory University in Atlanta, Georgia, conducted a study to see how epigenetics impacts cycles of addiction and mental illness in people living in the inner cities.[3] She discovered anecdotal evidence that suggests a transfer of risk from one generation to another and how difficult it is to break that cycle.

She and her colleague Brian Dian studied genetic inheritance using lab mice. They wanted to see if mice passed on a fear reaction to their grandpups. Their research revealed that genetic imprints from traumatic experiences carry through at least two generations. Certain fears can be inherited through the generations. A chemical scent was introduced to the mouse environment, and every time the mice smelled it, they received an electric shock until they associated the smell with the shock. Ressler and Dian discovered that the same reaction was then passed on to their pups, even though the pups were never shocked and only smelled the chemical. The third generation of pups— grandchildren of the original mice—also shuddered in fear without being shocked.

According to the *New York Times* article by Carl Zimmer, "The Famine Ended Seventy Years Ago, but Dutch Genes Still Bear Scars," a study was conducted

---

[3] https://www.scientificamerican.com/article/fearful-memories-passed-down/

during WWII on pregnant women in the Netherlands during a time of famine and the impact it had on their children.[4]

In September of 1944, the Dutch railway workers decided to strike, hoping it would stop Nazi troops from using the rails and helping the Allied forces. The Nazis decided to retaliate and block food supplies causing the country to experience a terrible famine. More than 20,000 people starved to death.

Referred to as the Dutch Hunger Winter, pregnant women and their children in utero during the famine were studied throughout their lives to see how they were impacted. As adults, these children were heavier than average, had higher cholesterol levels and experienced higher levels of obesity, diabetes and schizophrenia. Those in utero during the famine also died earlier than those who were born before or after the Dutch Hunger Winter. They experienced a 10 percent increase in mortality after the age of sixty-eight, according to Dr. Lumey.

While your cells share the same genes, some are active, and some are silent. They discovered that the

---

[4] https://www.nytimes.com/2018/01/31/science/dutch-famine-genes.html

program on how the DNA would be expressed is largely locked into place before birth.

This is why we can have issues around food if a grandparent experienced a famine or scarcity if they lived through a depression. We all inherit these programs from our ancestors. Before you condemn your great-great-grandparent for your money issues, you also inherited their courage, strength and ability to be resilient during difficult times.

As Americans, we are almost all immigrants or children of immigrants. It's important to thank them and know that they were doing the best they could with what they had at the time. We may carry their pain in our DNA, but we also carry their gifts.

A study of Holocaust survivors finds trauma passed on in children's genes.[5] According to this study, they discovered that genetic changes stemming from the trauma suffered by Holocaust survivors were capable of being passed on to their children and subsequent generations.

The conclusion from a research team at New York's Mount Sinai hospital led by Rachel Yehuda studied

---

[5] https://www.theguardian.com/science/2015/aug/21/study-of-holocaust-survivors-finds-trauma-passed-on-to-childrens-genes

thirty-two Jewish men and women who had either been interned in a Nazi concentration camp, witnessed or experienced torture or who had had to hide during the second world war.

They compared the genes of their children, who are known to have an increased likelihood of stress disorders, with Jewish families who were living outside of Europe during the war. "The gene changes in the children could only be attributed to Holocaust exposure in the parents," said Yehuda.

The idea is controversial; however, our genes are modified by our environment all the time through chemical tags that attach themselves to our DNA, switching genes on and off. This switching impacts how the DNA is expressed in future generations.

Here is an example of a client of mine who is of Brazilian descent. Her family was part of a long line of indigenous healers or what many people refer to as medicine men and women. She had a natural ability to heal people, but for some reason, she had a deep belief that she would never be able to make a living as a healer. It haunted her because it was something that she longed to do, but something was blocking her. Because of her desire to help people, she worked in the pharmaceutical industry, but she was very unhappy. She longed to express her gifts and her passion of being a full-time healer.

We decided to do a guided meditation that would take her back through her subconscious mind and travel through her DNA to find out the root cause of her belief that she could never support herself as an herbalist or healer. During the guided meditation, she went back to an ancestor who was living in Brazil during the time that the Portuguese arrived.

The Portuguese were Catholic and didn't believe in working with the local healers. They thought of them as witch doctors. They knew that the belief in these native healers ran deep, so they came up with the idea that if they were truly healers, then their abilities must come from God. Therefore, if gifts came from God, the indigenous healers should not be allowed to charge for healings.

In my client's meditation, she watched her ancestors starve; they had no other way to support themselves. They had to stop doing their work full time, and slowly through the generations, they stopped working as healers. Even though she had the gifts and desires, the belief that she could not charge for her healing services was so strong that it kept her from her dream. During the guided meditation, when she saw her ancestor in so much pain, she could talk to her ancestor and offer her a healing.

Once her ancestor was healed, that energetically switched the DNA expression in my client, and she ended up quitting her job and going into the healing profession. Her DNA was not altered. Her beliefs altered the way her DNA is expressed.

I recently spoke to a man who spent most of his first forty years of life wanting to die. He spoke about how painful it was to not want to be on this earth anymore but had never personally experienced any real trauma. He said that he repeatedly attempted suicide and had no idea why. I asked him if any family members had experienced any trauma, and he mentioned that he was Jewish and that his father had survived the Holocaust. He told me how his father was a survivor of the German occupation of Western Belorussia. German SS created Ghettos and would go in and liquidate most of the inhabitants. Those who survived left the ghettos and survived as nomads in the Naliboki Forest for several years.

Can I prove that this was the reason my friend didn't want to live from the time of his earliest memories until the age of forty? No. We may never know the reason. It is hard to explain why a young boy would come into this world in so much pain, attempting suicide for so many years of his life without any explanation as to why.

Have you thought about how to discover the Lies you have inherited from your ancestors? Start by looking at beliefs, behaviors, or physical symptoms that don't seem to make sense to you or are patterns in your family. You and your family members just might be taking on a Lie from your great-great-grandparent. If you want to know more about epigenetics, one of my favorite books on the subject is Mark Wolynn's book, *It didn't Start With You*, which discusses how inherited family trauma shapes who we are and how to end the cycle.

Don't forget, inherited beliefs aren't always bad. It took a lot of courage to leave a country, language, and culture behind to come to a new land. It took certain skills that were learned over many years that may have been handed down to you. We often think that inherited beliefs we take on are Lies, but leadership, courage, love or art, and music could have come from an ancestor, too, and those could be part of your Truth.

Chapter Eight

The Lie That You Can Solve Your Problem Without Doing Anything Differently

"We can't solve problems by using the same kind of thinking we used when we created them." Albert Einstein

Every person and every circumstance is a mirror for us to see what we need to heal. As humans, we often have the inability to see ourselves. In order to see what I need to work on, I look at the circumstances, people, and lessons that keep reappearing in my life. I go inward and ask myself, *What is this person teaching me? Why are they in my life? What can I do differently to resolve my situation this time?*

When I am triggered by someone or something, I try not to make it about them because no one can make me feel anything without my permission. So I ask myself, *What is unresolved in my belief system? What Lie has not been let go of or forgiven?*

Changing the way we deal with a trigger or beliefs that are Lies is how we begin to get off the hamster wheel of doing the same thing over and over while expecting a different result. We all tend to have routines. What happens when we mix things up? We get uncomfortable. Discomfort is our friend. While our subconscious is busy trying to keep us safe by compelling us to desire the familiar, a part of us longs for something different—a different way of seeing a person, situation, or belief. Neuroplasticity means that your brain can rewire itself when you change your mindset. Sounds easy, right?

Do you have a favorite seat at the dinner table, a favorite side of the bed, a morning ritual, or even the same exact drive to work every morning? When a guest comes over and inadvertently sits in your chair, how do you feel? When an accident happens on your way to work, and you get rerouted, how do you feel? We are creatures of habit, and our beliefs are part of our habits; we get comfortable with them. Change can take time.

Many techniques can help you reprogram your Lies faster, but you must have a desire to change. If you don't want to release your lies—the beliefs that no longer serve you—you won't. Why wouldn't someone want to get rid of a Lie that doesn't serve them? There is always a benefit to holding onto the Lie or behavior. It's serving them in some way; otherwise, a person wouldn't hold onto it.

For example, think of someone who may be chronically ill or often gets into accidents. This person realizes that he gets something out of staying unwell. Possibly he receives attention, people taking care of him, checking in on him more often, buying him things, doing things for him, and even paying for things for or financially supporting him. Sometimes this can be very comforting. And, likely, if you ever tell this person that you suspect they are doing this, you will be met with denial.

Most of those behaviors are unconscious, yet the chronic pain or consistent accidents are real. It's important not to belittle the person's pain. Instead, talk to him about what it might be like to release his pain and have his life back. Encourage other ways of releasing the pain or other issues beyond how they are doing it now.

Being responsible for your own life is not always easy. It requires actually stepping into your power, and not everyone is ready for that. Therefore, for some people, it remains easier to live a Lie.

People often give their power away to their circumstances to entice others to do things for them.

When it's time to release the pain, go to rehab, and start doing things for themselves, they get worse or stop progressing. They may get depressed and start to feel like a victim. Others step in, enable them and perpetuate Lies of helplessness and inability to change.

One of Alcoholics Anonymous (AA) tenets is that to get healthy and stay sober, part of their recovery process is to be of service. Why is service so important in AA? Service helps others with problems and reminds the individual of where they have come from. Helping others takes the focus off the individual. This is important because many of the alcoholic's problems arise from self-absorption.

Being of service is part of our DNA. It's who we are. We find joy in being of service to others. The important thing is finding the balance between being of service to others and being of service to self. Make sure that your needs are met.

According to an article in Forbes, Evan Carmichael believes if you're not happy, it is because you're not serving. It's why he wrote a book called *Built to Serve*.[6] According to Evan, "I think people can tend to be more

---

[6] https://www.forbes.com/sites/garrettgunderson/2020/09/08/serving-others-is-as-important-as-food-and-sex/?sh=346f72597ede

selfish in difficult times, as they focus on survival. But, the key may be instead to serve."

The need to serve is even backed up by science. Functional MRIs show that the brain areas that light up during acts of service are the same parts that light up when the brain is focused on food or sex.

We often have a part of us that sabotages us. At one point in time, I had a voice inside of me that constantly put me down. I was so good at convincing myself I would fail that I created a Lie that it was impossible to believe in myself.

Have you ever heard of the saying, "I'll kill you before you kill me?" My voice said, "I'll kill me before you kill me." I didn't mean it literally; it was a way to sabotage myself before someone could criticize me.

A part of us unconsciously keeps us from reaching our goals. How does an unconscious part sabotage us? Have you ever gone on a diet and had a really great day where all day long you ate healthfully and then, after dinner, had a pint of ice cream? We have younger wounded versions of ourselves that run the show—the little girl or the little boy who needs comfort. We can use addiction to sabotage ourselves, live with imposter syndrome, feel like a fraud, start a fight with someone, or blame our problems on someone else.

Mindset is everything when you want to improve.

Carol Dweck started a movement with her book called the *Growth Mindset*. According to Carol, a growth mindset is when "... people believe that their most basic abilities can be developed through dedication and hard work—brains and talent are just the starting point. This view creates a love of learning and a resilience that is essential for great accomplishment."

A fixed mindset means you believe you are born with certain intelligence, talents, and abilities that are innate and cannot be changed. You are simply born with a talent. If you're not good at something, you will think you will never be good at it and often give up. A growth mindset means that talents and abilities can be developed. Your mindset plays a major role in motivation, resilience, and achievement. Being flexible and having a positive mindset are critical to a growth mindset. When you are fearful and inflexible or think you already have the answers to something, you will block your progress and success. You also block your free will.

When I moved to New Hampshire, I didn't know anyone, so I intentionally attended as many networking groups as possible. I was invited to speak at one particular women's group. The meeting started with a time for each of us to introduce ourselves, and after that introduction period, I'd give my presentation.

I had recently trained in something called Thinner Band Hypnosis, where clients are hypnotized to think that they have had gastric band surgery. This technique helps the client feel full and curbs the desire to eat, so weight loss often happens faster than just dieting alone. I was also trained as an energy medicine practitioner, along with many other things.

I introduced myself and told everyone that I was a hypnotherapist specializing in weight loss and practiced energy medicine. Pretty unique, right? Who knew sitting right next to me was a woman named Sue who did the exact same thing as I did! She stood up and told everyone that she was a hypnotherapist specializing in weight loss, and she also worked in energy medicine.

I broke out in a sweat. The Lie I told myself was that no one would want to work with me. Sue had been with this organization for a while, and everyone knew her. After her introduction, she looked at me with her wise eyes and said to me, "Well then, what are the odds of this? There will be plenty of opportunities for both of us. You do things that I don't do, and I do things that you don't do. I bet we are going to end up referring to each other."

That was over ten years ago, and we continue to be friends to this day. Years later, we still refer to each other, talk to each other regularly, and always have a good laugh.

Reframing

Reframing is one of the most powerful ways of changing your Lies, and it's a huge part of having a growth mindset. My fire walk story is a perfect example of a reframe. I was convinced I was going to die, have my feet amputated, or end up in the hospital with severe burns. When my friend looked at me and asked me how many feet of fire I had already walked during our week-long training, it changed the way I saw the forty feet of red-hot coals.

Even though I hadn't walked the forty feet all at once like my graduation walk, I had walked seven to ten feet of fire every night for five nights in a row. He helped me see that I had already walked over forty feet of fire and that I could do it. It was no longer impossible in my mind. Reframing is a gift you can use for anything you find challenging or may be afraid of accomplishing.

Here's another illustration of reframing. According to the article "The Missing Bullets and Abraham Wald" by Chris Dobbert, during WWII, fighter planes often returned from battle riddled with bullet holes.[7] Researchers found the most commonly damaged areas and sought to reinforce them, which, in turn, created a weight issue. Extra metal on the planes weighed them down and made them slower and less maneuverable. Yet it was imperative to enhance the armor in the places with the greatest need.

Abraham Wald, a mathematician, pointed out a way to reframe this data. Looking at this information from another perspective offered an entirely different solution. Maybe the planes that weren't covered in bullet holes in those areas weren't coming home? Maybe the planes that returned were getting shot in less critical areas—the wings, for example—thus enabling their return. Perhaps the planes shot in critical areas—in the engine, for example—simply couldn't return. That

---

[7] https://medium.com/@christian.dobbert/the-missing-bullet-holes-and-abraham-wald-25c68d7a870f

insight changed the trajectory of armoring fighter planes.

When you look at information from different angles, there is an entirely different story to tell.

Exercise

Imagine a scenario that is very painful for you to think about.

What are the assumptions you are making about what happened?

How could you reframe it in a more positive way?

When you reframe it, do you feel better about it?

Let It Go!

Holding onto pain is something many of us do really well. Frequently it feels like it's too painful to look at, feel, or deal with. By stuffing your feelings down, you prolong your agony. You think that you are not feeling the pain, but inevitably, it will show up in other ways, and often, unfortunately, in ways you may not associate with the original issue. When we suppress Lies and negative feelings, they have to go somewhere. They can be stored in your cells, create habits and addiction, or even stress and anxiety.

A client came to me with a desire to quit smoking. His father died forty years previously when the client was twelve years old. The client's uncle brought him to the funeral and offered him a cigarette to help him feel better. The client then began using cigarettes as a way to suppress his grief unconsciously.

Cigarettes impact the heart and lung area where grief is stored; that area is where the heart chakra is. (A chakra is a Sanskrit word that means wheel. We have seven major chakras along our spine.) The reason why he couldn't quit smoking all of these years was that he had unprocessed grief.

When I asked his subconscious mind to take me to the root cause of his smoking, it took us right to the moment his uncle gave him the cigarette at his father's funeral. I had my client release the grief he held for a lifetime. After years of not being able to quit smoking, he let go of the Lie that it was not possible to quit smoking.

One of my clients was in high school and dealt with immense pressure. He was in two varsity sports simultaneously—skiing and swimming—applying to colleges and trying to increase his SAT scores to get into his dream school. That particular year was very icy on the ski slopes. He had a terrible fear of ice, and he was worried about how he would perform for the team. He told himself the Lie that he would let the team down.

I worked with him to get over his fear of icy slopes. While I was working with him, I helped him let go of his anxiety about taking the SATs. He was waitlisted at his number one choice, and the school informed him that he needed to raise his score by seventy-five points. I don't know about you, but I don't remember my test scores going up that much each time I took my SATs.

We worked on his stress and anxiety. We determined that eighty percent of his thoughts were focused on his anxiety. Because of that, not much was left to focus on the task at hand. Once he released his anxiety, it opened up his ability to focus and concentrate. The more energy and focus he had for his tasks, the better he performed. He began winning his ski races regardless of slope conditions, and he increased his SATs and was accepted to his top choice college.

I have a wonderful mentor, Dr. Al Tatarusus—also known as Dr. Al—who is a true renaissance man. At the time of writing this book, he was ninety-six years old, still going to church, composing music, and living in Naples, Florida. He wears a ponytail and drives a Mercedes convertible. We became fast friends about eight years ago when I saw him speak at a conference, at the age of eighty-eight. Dr. Al is a graduate of Harvard, a Certified Hypnotherapist, composer of classical music, singer, and organ player. He loves to teach, and he loves to color his talks with foul language to keep people's attention.

One day he called me and told me that his daughter—who was a physician in Boston, Massachusetts—fell in the subway station and smacked her head on the concrete. She was in the hospital, and the doctors were trying to stop her brain from hemorrhaging. He told me how he sat awake at 2:00 a.m., wondering if it was in his best interest to worry all night. He decided it wasn't. He then asked if it was in his daughter's best interest for him to worry all night. He decided it wasn't.

When I lived in New Hampshire, I spent a lot of time with Dr. Al. He transformed my personal life and the work I do with my clients. I didn't realize how much I worried about everything. I didn't know that when you worry about someone else, you send them an energetic message that you don't believe that they can accomplish their goals. When you worry, you focus on all the bad things that could happen and will likely never occur.

Dr. Al trained me in a technique called the Emotional Release Method. He spent two hours trying to get me to release the need to worry. I couldn't let it go. My Lie was that I didn't know what I would possibly think about if I let go of the need to worry. After an exhausting two hours, he finally looked at me and said, "Lisa, you're a relatively intelligent woman, don't you think?"

I responded, yes.

He then added, "Don't you think that if something ever did go wrong, you would be able to figure it out?"

I responded, yes.

He then looked me straight in the eye and said, "Then *let it go!*"

I finally let it go. I let go of my Lie, and then, for two weeks, I walked around in a fog, trying to figure out what to think about. All of a sudden, new thoughts began to come into mind. I became more creative. I was no longer dedicating eighty percent of my thoughts to something that may never happen. I began thinking about manifesting and creating the life I wanted.

This story reminds me of my favorite skit with Bob Newhart on MadTV where he plays a therapist trying to help his client who has a fear of being buried in a box. He asked her if anyone had ever tried to bury her in a box, she replied, no, but thinking about it makes my life horrible.

He responded, what you are saying is that you are claustrophobic?

She replied, yes, yes, that's it. Bob Newhart looks at her and tells her that he has two words for her and he wants her to listen to them very, very carefully. I want you to take them out of the office with you and incorporate them into your life. Stop it! S-T-O-P it! She responds, so I should just stop it? He responds, yes, just stop it! I belly laugh every time I watch that skit. Two simple words, yet not so easy. That's why having powerful techniques and tools are critical in changing your beliefs which will then change your thoughts and behaviors.

Challenge the Lies

I recently saw the actress Salma Hayek on a video talking about the idea of being insulted. She used the example that if someone cursed at you in another language, you wouldn't know what they were saying. She said that though they could be saying the meanest things to you, you would have no idea, so you might even laugh at them.

We allow words—the words we say to ourselves and what we hear from others—to have such incredible meaning. Words affect our thoughts, and those thoughts influence our behavior. However, if you don't allow yourself to embody the Lie, it won't impact you.

A professional golfer once told me that he couldn't putt. Yet, when he first began playing professionally, putting was the best part of his game. Twenty years before he came to see me, he went to a tournament, had a bad day, and just couldn't get his act together, especially his putting. After the tournament, someone walked up to him and said, "Gee, it's too bad that you don't know how to putt because if you did, you would be a phenomenal golfer."

After he heard and absorbed that Lie, he stopped being able to putt. He became known as the golf pro who couldn't putt. We spent an hour together, and he released the Lie. After our session, he went to the golf course and played nine holes. He called me in disbelief that he had just played the best game in years.

When we have bad days like that, we can do one of two things. We can brush it off and tell ourselves it was an off day, or we can take it on as true. No matter how much of an expert we are in something, we don't always do our best. The best thing we can do to recover from a bad day is to learn from it, forgive ourselves and let it go.

When we take on a belief created on a bad day, especially unconsciously, we don't have access to it. We don't realize the impact it's having on us. We get frustrated and angry at ourselves, and that little voice inside our heads that thinks it's protecting us will sabotage us and make up new Lies to ensure our actions match our beliefs. That's why we often end up on a hamster wheel doing the same things over and over, expecting a different result.

We have to access the Lie at the root in order to change it and transform it into our Truth. Sounds easy, right? Unfortunately, it's hard to access those Lies. The Lies are stored deep in your unconscious mind. By using Hypnosis, NLP, or the Emotional Release Method—as a few examples of many techniques available—you can access these Lies and transform them.

When I first moved out on my own to start my life over again, I moved to a log home on the side of a mountain near a ski area on eighteen acres. Why would someone terrified of being alone decide to move somewhere where they didn't know a soul, had no support system, and had to deal with harsh weather conditions?

I have learned throughout my life that fear is one of my greatest teachers. When I am afraid of something, I know I have to do it. It's why I took the week-long fire walking course. When you live in harsh climates, your home and property take a beating, and you need to repair your home more often. Log homes are what I consider living, breathing organisms. They expand and contract with the weather, and occasionally you will hear a snap, crackle, and pop. One day I took a look at my deck and realized that it needed refinishing.

I had never used an electric power tool before. My ex-husband was very handy and always took care of those kinds of projects. I suddenly wished that I had paid more attention to him when he repaired things around the house. The deck was twelve hundred square feet, and I knew that this would be an expensive project if I hired someone to do it. I decided to conquer my fear of using power tools and do it myself.

I bought a power washer, borrowed a friend's belt sander, went to the hardware store and asked the clerk to fix me up with everything I needed. I put on knee pads, safety goggles, and a mask and started sanding.

I will never forget the first day; I sanded one entire side of the wrap-around deck. I was exhausted, covered in sweat and sawdust. All of a sudden, I heard thunder in the distance. I looked up at the sky and saw huge black clouds headed toward me. I panicked because I was told that you couldn't let the wood get wet between sanding and staining. If it rained, I would have to re-sand the entire side I had just completed, and all of my hard work would have been a waste.

I prayed for a second wind of energy because I was exhausted. I grabbed the stain and a staining pad with a long handle. I started staining while praying the rain would pass by and not come near my house. I got a third of the way through staining, and the pole attached to the staining pad snapped in half. Now I had to get on my hands and knees and continue the job. It was evening at this point, and the sky was getting darker and darker. I could barely see what I was doing, but I got the side stained.

As soon as I finished, I noticed that the clouds were no longer there, and all I saw were twinkling stars. The next morning, I took a look at my work, and it was a mess. I knew that I would have to put a second coat on anyway, but I felt enormous pride in my work. Something inside of me changed after I stained that deck. I realized that I had told myself a lie about what I could and could not accomplish. I love the work I did on that deck, it's still holding up, and I will do it again when it's time.

One of the things that I love about living here in Vermont is how many women I know who are incredibly independent and empowered. They drive giant tractors, clear their own land, cut down trees with chainsaws, drive trucks with plows, manage farms, shoot guns and plow driveways. I grew up in a suburb of New Jersey, regularly traveling to New York City to shows and museums; I was not raised to do those things these local women do. The lie I told myself was that I couldn't ever do anything like that. These women are true inspirations to me, and I feel so lucky to be in their company.

I have stopped limiting my thinking and creating Lies about what I can and cannot do. I am surrounded by women who have traveled and worked around the world and have chosen a simpler life in nature, living close to the land. I love my life, my friends, and the mountain views.

When Does This Not Work?

Not everyone is open to change. Why? There is power in pride and control. It's about the devil you know. It's not easy to admit when you are wrong or admit the way you see the world is wrong or skewed. The idea of being humiliated can be too much to bear.

One of my mentors, Tucano Nonni, said that people with too much pride could not make a mistake, show weakness, or even show their love to others. Pride will take you out of authenticity, what is true, block change, freeze your evolution, and therefore block true transformation. Think about a tree in a hurricane. Which trees survive? The ones that are rigid with shallow roots or the trees that are flexible?

When I sense a person is prideful, I sometimes ask, "Would you rather be right or be happy?" This prompts them to think. It's also important to give someone an easy way out to admit they are wrong and acknowledge the slightest shift from a place of gratitude. Thank them for being open, and establish trust between the two of you by acknowledging how hard that must have been for them to see that as a possibility. Create a safe place to let them have their feelings.

People need a safe place to express and process a Lie they have embodied for a lifetime. Allow space for them to feel raw and vulnerable. Never say I told you so! That is the fastest way to shut someone down. Saying I told you so offers nothing but making you feel better and leaving them feeling shame.

Chapter Nine

The Lie That When You Forgive, It Makes What They Did Okay

The Power of Forgiveness

Practicing forgiveness is one of the single most powerful things you can do. I remember watching examples of people whose loved ones were killed, and these people stood up and forgave the perpetrators in the courtroom. I never understood how and why someone would have the capacity to do that.

However, as I have gotten older, I have begun to realize the importance of forgiveness. It is not about telling the other person that what they did is okay. It is deciding not to carry the pain anymore. Holding onto resentment is like swallowing a poison pill and expecting the other person to die. Most of the time, the other person is not even thinking about you, and you end up spending hours feeling hateful, angry, and resentful, and that affects your thoughts and your physical body.

About a year ago, my business partner, Kevin Martin, introduced me to Ho'oponopono, an ancient Hawaiian forgiveness practice, and boy is it powerful. He created a group that would meet weekly, and everyone in the group would check in with miracles that happened in their lives from the act of forgiveness.

Kevin told me the amazing story of Dr. Ihaleakala Hew Len. He attended the University of Colorado and received his degree in Psychology. He then graduated from the University of Utah with a MS degree in special education and a doctorate from the University of Iowa. He was also a spiritual expert who practiced the ancient ritual of Ho'oponopono. Ho'oponopono is a legendary Hawaiian healing and cleansing method that focuses on healing through loving oneself.

Dr. Hew Len was hired by a prison in Hawaii to counsel people in the wing of the prison that housed the criminally insane. He took the job on the condition that he only looked through the files of each patient and did not see anyone in person. At first, the prison system thought he was joking and dismissed his request and refused to hire him. After several months of trying to hire a psychologist, they were desperate enough to hire him. While reviewing the records, he chanted a mantra over each individual file. Dr. Hew Len did this over and over for months.

What's interesting about Dr. Hew Len's approach is that the patients had no idea that this was happening, and they were never asked to repeat the mantra themselves. He believed that because we all share a connection to each other, we have the ability to impact each other positively or negatively. We all have the power to heal by our own actions and motivations. His humility ultimately led to healing his patients.[8]

I recently watched a movie called, *The Railway Man* starring Colin Firth and Nicole Kidman. I found it to be the ultimate story of forgiveness. It is the story of a former British Army officer who was tortured as a prisoner of war during World War II at a Japanese labor camp. Horrible nightmares haunted him, and he had terrible PTSD. He lived with the memories of the horrific images of what he witnessed and his own torture. He discovered that the man responsible for much of the horrific brutality was still alive, and he set out for revenge.

Spoiler Alert! The army officer decides to travel to Japan, where he desires to confront and kill his nemesis.

---

[8] https://breeganjane.com/lessons-from-hooponopono

When he arrived at the Japanese man's place of work, he realized that the man was a tour guide at the camp. He was also haunted by what occurred and what he was responsible for. The British soldier ultimately had compassion for him, and they eventually became close friends.

When you carry resentment, the only person it upsets is you. Imagine you are carrying a backpack of bowling balls formed from resentment, bitterness, and anger. It would be a heavy pack to bear. As you forgive, you let go of the bowling balls and lighten the load. You feel free and light.

When you are triggered, you are literally giving your power away to the person you are angry at. Imagine when all of your thoughts or a large percentage of your thoughts go to thinking about someone else; what is left for you? What amount of thoughts go into your ability to have peace, create, and love. Every thought you have produces neuropeptides that move throughout your body and attach to your cells.

When you create a Lie, you are negatively programming your cells. What happens when you spend years thinking negatively? I don't care if it's about the world, about a person, or an event; continued negative thoughts create resentment. Resentment, gone unchecked, will create many different types of problems for you, including physical, mental, and emotional.

So, what do you do? Is it okay for others to do bad things? Am I supposed to walk around and pretend something didn't happen? No. Just because you forgive does not imply that what the other person did was okay. You don't have to like them, but if you have the mindset that everyone is doing the best they can with what they have, then you are on your way to forgiveness.

If someone was abused as a child, that is what they know about the world. This is the lens through which they see the world. If he doesn't do any work on himself to shift and change the pattern and lies created, he will repeat the pattern, and that pattern can be passed down generationally. Remember, much of our own limiting beliefs and behaviors come from our unconscious. The younger versions of ourselves don't realize what they are doing. That does not excuse the behavior.

The world will react to bad behavior and your lies over and over. You can choose to change and forgive, or you can continue the cycle of pain. Whatever you choose, know that once you have made a choice, you are not a victim. You have chosen to either continue or discontinue the cycle. One day when you are ready to let go and forgive, you will feel lighter and more free.

Chapter Ten

By Finding Your Truth, You Will Learn to Believe in Yourself, Discover Your Values, Trust Your Instincts and Eliminate Your Lies

"Happiness is not the absence of problems; it's the ability to deal with them." Steve Maraboli

Have you ever thought about the fact that we choose our thoughts? We choose every moment. Your subconscious mind will choose thoughts and emotions to protect you, even if at the same time they sabotage you. There are no neutral thoughts; all of them have a purpose. With practice, you can learn to redirect your thoughts. Refocus your thoughts on where you want your life to go.

How often do we attempt to do something, change our minds, and later discover that the original thought was the right thing to do. Those decisions sometimes haunt us for long periods of time. We often have really great instincts, and we let others talk us out of them. It's important to trust ourselves, our gifts, and our skills.

We encounter and live with problems throughout our lives. Most people think that in order to be happy, you can't have problems. That is the farthest thing from the truth. It's about having the capacity to deal with problems, as well as your attitude in dealing with them. Something only becomes a problem if you make it a problem.

I rarely go wrong when I trust my instincts. When people ask me how I made a particular decision, I always answer, "Because it felt right. I close my eyes, and I feel it. I check in to see if it feels good and expansive or if I feel pulled to do it."

I don't always know why I am supposed to do something when I feel that pull. Often, I don't know until after I do something why I was supposed to make that decision. Sometimes making decisions this way can be scary. However, the more I have learned to trust that feeling, the less afraid I am of my decisions.

I started out waiting for information to come to me three times. For instance, if there is a book I should read, I might hear someone mention it in passing, then I will turn on the TV, and the author is being interviewed on a television show, and then someone may recommend it to me in passing. I remember how excited I used to get waiting for my three signs. After a while, I started to recognize the feeling I would get from the confirmation of the three signs the first time I heard something. I began trusting that feeling more and more.

When I was in the process of separating from my ex, I struggled with the decision of where I was going to live. I didn't want to keep the family home; it held too many memories for me. I started looking at apartments in the town we were living in. Nothing felt right. I went to Vermont for the weekend, and I knew I had to move there. I didn't know a soul; I would have to start my business over from scratch and start my life over at the age of fifty-four. Even though it made more sense for me to stay local, it didn't feel right. It wasn't easy to move, but once I got there, I knew I had made the right decision.

The Truth in Knowing Your Why and Your Purpose

We come into this world alone. We are here to experience joy. How can we experience joy if we don't love and appreciate ourselves? Sometimes we put pressure on relationships expecting others to make us happy, but that often turns into a recipe for disaster. If we don't fully see ourselves, how can we love ourselves?

When you discover *why* you are here, it helps you better understand who you are and what brings you joy. Many personality tests exist, and one I like is the DISC test—dominance, influence, steadiness, and compliance. It's a personality test based on your behavior. Other excellent tests include the Meyers Briggs test, Predictive Index test, and many more. They are all valuable and tell you *how* you do something, *how* you relate to others, and *how* you behave but have you ever truly understood *why* you do something?

About two years ago, I met someone offering a marketing challenge, and as part of the challenge, she helped people discover their Why. I initially wondered why knowing my Why would help me in my life. I was a bit skeptical. When I received my results from the Why Institute, my life changed.

Daniel Dominguez, Chief Growth Officer of the WHY Institute, stepped me through the different why's and helped me discover my *Why*, *How*, and *What*, also known as my WHY.os (WHY operating system).

I discovered that my Why is Challenge. I challenge conventional thinking. I love to think outside the box and help others develop solutions that no one has ever thought of. It's a bit of a high for me, honestly. Helping others develop new solutions and challenge norms comes easily and effortlessly for me. As someone who grew up being different—learning differently than others, being artistic and creative, questioning things in the world, and searching for meaning and the purpose of life—I am not mainstream in my thinking. Who else would walk on red-hot coals, walk on broken glass, break arrows and rebar with their throat in order to have the courage to change their life? I needed a challenge! Through the years, being out of the mainstream has created a great deal of pain for me. I've lost friends, family, and relationships over my beliefs and values.

I have discovered it is essential for me to know my values and better understand why I am here. This awareness helps me find joy, gives me confidence that I'm going in the right direction, and helps me understand and accept myself and find my Truth.

Before I discovered my Why I sometimes felt broken for not fitting in, it was hard when people didn't understand me.

When I tried to market my business and talk about what I did, people looked at me like I had two heads. I realized that I was marketing to the wrong people, and I discovered that I had to speak to people like me, who are different and like to think outside the box. They don't have to be challenging personalities; they just need to be comfortable thinking outside the box. Those people get me, trust me, and want to work with me. They feel safe with me because they know that I understand them and will never ask them to try and fit in. I honor and accept people who are unique and different. I also honor people who are more conventional in their thinking, and because of that, I know that I have to taper my language so they feel comfortable around me. For example, I might say I offer guided meditations instead of hypnosis. When you know who you are talking to by knowing their why you can use their language and understand what motivates them.

When I took the WHY test, I learned that not only was my why Challenge, but my How is Better Way and my What is Make Sense. I Challenge conventional thinking, help people find a Better Way, and bring the ability to Make Sense out of complicated situations and problems—Why, How, and What. I sat with my test results and looked at how I lived my life. I realized that my Why is not solely based on work. It can be, but it also creates a foundation for everything in life. Your Why existed before you had a job or family. Jobs and family are important considerations when making your life decisions, but they are not your Why.

When my business partner and I decided to start a business, we worked diligently on our messaging. We kept changing everything around, and nothing felt right. We put our website up, but our message didn't feel effective and compelling. After nine months in business, we both discovered our WHY.os. Ironically, they are almost the same. Kevin's is Challenge, Better Way, and Contribute. Once we knew what our individual Why's were, we could decide what the WHY.os of our business would be. Once we knew that, we had our revised website up in a week.

I have a client who has the why of Simplify in his WHY.os. He has this amazing ability to take very complex information from engineers and simplify their message into layman's terms. He can take a five-paragraph email from an engineer and reply in four bullet points.

He used to carry shame around his Why. He didn't know how to charge for his services. He was charging by the hour, and he wasn't making much money. I explained to him that he needed to change his fee structure based on his Why. He has the unique gift of simplifying information in order to bring products to the market for consumers. Consumers do not want the complicated details of how a product works; they just want to know how this product will change their lives.

According to The WHY Institute, there are nine Whys. Gary Sanchez, the founder of the WHY Institute, went to see Simon Sinek speak about the importance of finding your Why. He was blown away. He was so excited when Simon's talk was over that he walked up to Simon and asked him to help him find his Why. Simon said that he doesn't show people how to find their Why; he just tells them Why it's important to know their Why. Gary interviewed thousands of people over a ten-year span and distilled the information into nine Whys.

1) *Contribute*: This is the most common Why. These are the people you want on your team; they want to make a difference in the lives of others. Their challenge is that they can often give too much and drain themselves.

2) *Trust*: These people can be counted on; they are great at creating loyalty. But don't get on their bad side because if you do, they will cut you off, and you most likely will not get a second chance.

3) *Make Sense*: These people can make sense of complicated situations and problems. They often figure out the answer before others, so if this is your Why, it's really important not always to solve other people's problems; let others try to find solutions themselves.

4) *Better Way*: These people always find a better way and share it. They are entrepreneurs and visionaries. Their challenge is that they can't stop improving things, and they have a hard time choosing something because another choice may be better.

5) *Right Way*: These people believe that all things have a proper and correct way to be done. They thrive in an environment where they can create structure. Their challenge is sometimes being too rigid and not being flexible with others. They have the attitude, "My way or the highway."

6) *Challenge*: These people—like me—like to think differently and challenge the status quo. They are out-of-the-box thinkers. The challenge with that is that because they are different, they're not often understood. Knowing that about themselves and explaining to others

they are coming from an out-of-the-box perspective encourages others to do the same.

7) *Mastery*: This Why includes the smallest percentage of the population. They have an insatiable thirst for knowledge and want to learn as much as they can about a particular subject. They don't just learn the basics; they will do a deep dive and literally try and master the subject. Their challenge is that their current knowledge level will never feel good enough to them. They will try and create a Rolls-Royce when they only need a Volkswagen.

8) *Clarity*: These people are masterful communicators and always seek to be understood and make sure that you feel understood. They will ask many questions to ensure a full understanding, but their challenge is that their need to be understood can border on fanatical. They can sometimes come off as overbearing, explaining things repeatedly despite the fact that you have made it clear you understand them.

9) *Simplify*: These people make everyone's life easier. You want to make sure you have one of these people on your management team. They have the unique gift of reducing the number of tasks to accomplish anything. They like everything simplified and do not do well in chaos. These are the people who

notoriously can take the three-part WHY.os of others and help them put them together into one sentence.

Why do I feel it is essential to know your Why? I am a firm believer in living in your Why and purpose. I know that when I make any decision in my life, it has to fit into my WHY.os. If it isn't different, better, and it doesn't make sense, I won't enjoy it. Once you master the Whys, you will see how people live in their Whys. They will buy a car, vacation, or choose a partner all through their Why.

A Contribute person may buy a minivan; a Trust person might buy a Volvo, and a Challenge person most likely goes into a showroom and looks for a limited edition of a model or a car with a funky color. As I learn and understand my Why and the Why of my friends, colleagues, and clients, I feel more in control of my life and have the ability to build stronger relationships because I can now communicate with them in their language.

When you discover your WHY.os, it helps you live in your Truth. When you feel aligned, you are in integrity and know who you are. You cannot be swayed; you feel anchored. Many people who don't own their Why feel shame about their Why. When you know who you are, Why you are here, and where you are going, everything will begin to align for you.

Want to discover your Why? Contact me about doing your own Why Discovery!
www.peakperformancemindsetcoaching.com

Build the Lens of Your Dreams by Discovering Your Values

In order to build the lens of your dreams, you need to fully know who you are. As I have said throughout this book, we are all programmed unconsciously throughout our lives—by the television, teachers, culture, schools, politicians, demographics, and much more. There are techniques coming up in this book that will help you unravel your false beliefs. Once you know who you aren't, you will then be able to discover who you are.

In other words, do you know what you value? Intentionally spending time on uncovering my values was life-changing for me. If you think about it, are you most happy when you are working or hanging out with people and businesses that share similar values as you? If you are in a relationship or, better yet, a marriage with someone and you do not share the same values, your relationship may be doomed. When you don't know your values, how will you choose a partner? We often assume that other people share the same interests and believe in what we do, so sometimes we can be blindsided when someone's values are different from ours, which may lead to the end of that relationship. What is also very important to know is that you both share the same definition of a particular value.

You and your partner may share the value of being devoted to your family. To one person, that may mean spending valuable time with your family, nurturing each other, and attending events that are important to one another. To someone else, it may be the act of providing. Being a provider is essential in a family, but when it constantly trumps family time, it is not congruent with the other partner, and both partners feel lonely and underappreciated. Balance is vital, as is agreement.

You may also have a partner who says that their value is trust. Trust creates loyalty. If you are not trustworthy in your life, you don't feel comfortable speaking your truth about where you are and what you are doing. If you don't trust people and don't believe people are trustworthy, your relationship will most likely not work.

Knowing your values helps you live a vibrant, meaningful, and joyful life. When you are with people who share similar values, you are happier, relaxed and more passionate about being in their company. You feel more energized.

Have you ever been to an event, worked in a company, or socialized with people who do not share your values? It's not a fun experience, as a matter of fact, it can be miserable and will drain your energy. When I worked on Fashion Avenue in NYC, I was constantly astounded at how mean, angry and miserable people were and how they had no problem projecting their misery onto their employees and customers. I worked for a women's sportswear company where I was in sales and sold to small specialty stores. These were Mom and Pop stores who depended on their businesses to support themselves and their families.

One time the company received a shipment of merchandise from the factory overseas that included pants, a blazer, a blouse, and a pleated skirt. The skirt was supposed to be pleated, but it was far from it. The skirts were all like a wrinkled ball. They could not be salvaged. My employer decided that they would ship the skirts to their customers anyway and the customers would have to deal with it. I was horrified. I think I cried almost every day I worked there. The company line was that there was nothing wrong with the skirt and they were not going to take it back. I ended up getting fired from that company, not over that issue, but something else that I refused to go along with. I remember how relieved I was when I walked out the door of that company. It was one of my first jobs out of college and I left knowing that I had just learned everything not to do in business.

When you know your values, it helps you make decisions in all different parts of your life. Knowing your values before you go to work for a company, join a nonprofit, become friends with anyone, or even selecting a school you wish to attend is very important.

Below is a great exercise to help you uncover and discover your values. I learned this exercise from my friend Tish Marie Peletier. She ran a week-long marketing challenge, and as part of the challenge, she ran us through this exercise which helped me discover my Why. Discovering those things changed my life. Interestingly, I didn't actually change what I was doing; instead, this exercise confirmed that I was already following Why, my purpose, and I was consistent with my values. It gave me the confidence to take my work to another level because I now owned it.

Peak Performance Mindset Coaching
Exercise adapted from TAPROOT
Core Values Exercise

Determine your core values. From the list below, choose and write down every core value that resonates with you. Don't overthink your selections, As you read through the list, simply write down the worlds that feel live a core value to you and you and personality. If you think of a value you possess that is not on the list, be sure to write it down as well.

Abundance, Acceptance, Accountability, Achievement, Advancement, Adventure, Advocacy, Ambition, Appreciation, Attractiveness, Autonomy, Balance, Being the Best, Benevolence, Boldness, Brilliance, Calmness, Caring, Challenge, Charity, Cheerfulness, Cleverness, Community, Commitment, compassion, Cooperation, Collaboration, Consistency, Contribution, Creativity, Credibility, Cutlousity, Daring, Decisiveness, Dedication, Dependability, Diversity, Empathy, Encouragement, Enthusiasm, Ethics, Excellence, Expressiveness, Fairness, Family, Friendships, Flexibility, Freedom, Fun Generosity, Grace, Growth, Flexibility, Happiness, Health, Honesty, Humility, Humor, Inclusiveness, Independence, Individuality, Innovation, Inspiration, Independence, Individuality, Innovation, Inspiration, Intelligence,

Intuition, Joy, Kindness, Leadership, Learning, Love, Loyalty, Making a Difference, Motivation, Optimism, Open-Mindedness, Originality, Passion, Performance, Personal Development, Proactive, Professionalism, Quality, Recognition, Risk Taking, Safety, Security, Service, Spirituality, Stability, Peace, Perfection, Playfulness, Popularity, Power, Preparedness, Proactivity, Professionalism, Punctuality, Recognition, Relationships, Reliability, Resliance, Resourcefulness, Responsibility, Responsiveness, Security, Self-Control, Selflessness, Simplicity, Stability, Success, Teamwork, Thankfulness, Thoughtfulness, Traditionalism, Trustworthiness, Understanding, Uniqueness, Usefulness, Versatility, Vision, Warmth, Wealth, Well-being, Wisdom,

Group all similar values together from the list of values you just created. Group them in a way that makes sense to you, personally. Group them in what feels like a similar theme.

Create a maximum of five groupings, drop the least important.

See the example below:

1. Abundance, Growth, Wealth, Security, Freedom, Independence, flexibility, Peace
2. Acceptance, Compassion, Inclusiveness, Intuition, Kindness, Love, Making a Difference, Open-Mindedness, Trustworthiness, Relationships
3. Appreciation, Encouragement, Thankfulness, Thoughtfulness, Mindfulness
4. Balance, Health, Personal Development, Spirituality, Well-being
5. Cheerfulness, Fun, Happy, Inspiration, Joy, Optimism, Playfulness

3. Choose one word within each grouping that best represents the theme or label for the entire group. Again, do not overthink your labels. There are no right or wrong answers. You are defining the answer that is right for you. See the example below – the label chosen for the grouping is bolded.

1. Abundance, Growth, Wealth, Security, **Freedom**, Independence, flexibility, Peace

2. Acceptance, Compassion, Inclusiveness, Intuition, Kindness, Love, **Making a Difference**, Open-Mindedness, Trustworthiness, Relationships

3. Appreciation, Encouragement, Thankfulness, Thoughtfulness, **Mindfulness**

4. **Balance**, Health, Personal Development, Spirituality, Well-being

5. **Cheerfulness**, Fun, Happy, Inspiration, Joy, Optimism, Playfulness

Once you know your values, it is important to live by them. Most people talk about the idea of happiness. To be happy, you need to know your Why, How, and What, your values, and have free will. This enables you to live in integrity. When you live a life that is not yours and you don't have free will, you cannot experience joy. You can try all you want, and you can pretend and put a fake smile on your face. It works until it does not anymore. It will wear you down.

Let's take it a step further. You are here for a purpose. If you are not living your purpose and living up to your fullest potential, things will begin to shift in your life. You may be less likely to find joy, and the world will be less likely to conspire for you. It may feel like the world is conspiring against you.

When you stay at a job you hate because you feel trapped and are afraid to lose your security, you will discover that security evaporates when you are doing something you are not meant to do. You will start to receive taps on the shoulder, over and over again. Work will become more and more miserable until one day, you get laid off, fired, or something happens that makes you so mad that you will quit, and you will not have another job waiting for you.

When you listen to that feeling, that voice inside you that says leave, you will find that it is easier to make the changes in your own time and on your own schedule. You won't be left in shock holding a box with your belongings and two weeks' severance. If you are doing too much and avoiding what you are meant to do, you may find yourself suddenly getting into an accident or breaking a bone, and then you have no choice but to stop, be quiet and go inward.

People think that they can hide their feelings when they are miserable. If you are showing up at work and you hate what you do, hate your boss or coworkers, people will be able to tell that you are unhappy. You will not do a good job, and you will be in a bad mood. No one wants to be around someone who is grumpy, miserable, or sick all day. When you suppress your feelings and they have no place to go, you will also begin to break down your body. Stress causes over seventy percent of disease. When you are happier at work, you will be healthier, take fewer sick days, and be more productive.

When you pay attention, the world will be a better and happier place for you. Knowing who you are and why you are here makes it easier to find your Truth and live your Truth with full integrity. Change is not easy. I put myself through a week of hell to get the courage to change my life. Could I have done it sooner? Maybe. But maybe I was not ready. Maybe I was not meant to change my life then. I try not to have regrets in my life. When it is time to make a decision in my life, I think about being at the end of my life and ask myself if I would regret it if I had not at least tried something.

"The master in the art of living makes little distinction between his work and his play, his labor and his leisure, his mind and his body, his information and his recreation, his love and his religion. He hardly knows which is which. He simply pursues his vision of excellence in whatever he does, leaving others to decide whether he is

working or playing. To him, he's always doing both."

—— James A. Michener

What if you don't know what you want? You don't have to know what you want; you can just know the feeling you want. At night, before you go to bed, try to meditate on the feelings you want in your life. When you go to sleep, you will continue that feeling all night. In the morning, close your eyes and meditate on what you want your life to feel like to set the tone for the day. When difficulties come up in your day, redirect and know that you are one day closer to living in your Truth.

Chapter Eleven

The Truth is That the Universe Will Always Conspire For You

When you make a decision, it should feel aligned. You should feel congruent. I have always lived my life by using my feelings as a barometer. When I moved to New Hampshire, I didn't know anyone and had to start my business over again. My goal was to have an office on Main Street. In Concord eventually.

However, being new to town with no established clientele, I was nervous about taking on an office with expensive rent and going into debt. I set the intention to share an office until I established myself, and then I would have my office on Main Street. At a networking event, I met a woman who had an office and only used it on nights and weekends. It was the perfect size, and she was part of a wellness center in a town twenty minutes from downtown Concord.

I thought this would be a great opportunity to meet people, establish myself, and pay low rent. It worked out really well for a year, and one morning, three clients in a row—remember my old sign of looking for three's—mentioned an available office on Main Street in Concord. When I explored the option, I saw the rent was four times what I was currently paying, and I was nervous about looking at it. I decided to trust and visit the spot to experience how it felt. I walked into the room, and I fell in love with the space. It felt like home. The voice in my head screamed how are you going to pay for this? My heart said go for it! I decided to go for it. The first month I was in my new space in Concord on Main Street, I broke even, and my business continued to grow from there.

I have always had the philosophy of trusting that everything is in divine order and that magic and miracles always happen in my life. Having a growth mindset and being flexible helps. If you are fixed on the idea of how something is meant to be and rigid about it, you may miss some really amazing opportunities. I have many stories of miracles in my life, and I bet you do too. You just have to know how to see things.

During the summer of 1983, I was a college student living just outside of Boston. I worked at a local clothing store and took a marketing class at Boston College to make up some credits for a class that didn't go very well during the school year. My ex-husband, then-boyfriend, worked at the Mountain View House in the White Mountains of New Hampshire. At the time, it was a very old grand inn that apparently, Stephen King was inspired to write the book *The Shining* while staying there as a guest.

One Friday evening, around sunset, I decided to head up to New Hampshire to visit for the weekend. About halfway there, I experienced my very first flat tire. I was a clueless twenty-year-old who had no idea how to change a flat and thought the best thing to do was pull over to the side of the highway and cry. This was way before cell phones, and I felt lost. Moments later, two cars pulled up behind me. A woman walked up to me and asked me if I had any cash on me. I was a college student, so the obvious answer was no. She proceeded to tell me how she had gotten a flat tire the week before, and no one would take her out-of-state check. She also informed me that a new tire would cost seventy dollars, and it would be best if I had cash—this was also before ATM machines. She handed me seventy dollars and told me to write her a check for the same amount. She took my check, and she was gone. I remember thinking that a grown woman should know better than to take a check from a college student, though in my case, the check was actually good.

After the woman left, a young man offered to change my flat tire. He looked at my spare tire, which was one of those little donut spares that allowed just enough driving miles to get you to a mechanic to buy a new tire. He put the spare on but let me know that everything was closed, and the farther north I went, the less opportunity I would have to find a new tire to purchase. He happened to work at a Dunkin Donuts just off the next exit, and his friend owned the gas station across the street. He called his friend who had closed up for the night and was about to head home and asked him if he would open the shop for me. His friend agreed. We drove over to the gas station, and he happened to have the exact tire I needed. Guess how much the new tire was? Exactly seventy dollars.

As I said earlier in the book, it is not always a straight line between where you are and where you want to go. Perseverance, trust, belief in oneself, and action are key.

As a child in school, I remember my teachers saying, do not tell me what you feel; tell me what you think. I believe that is such a great disservice to children. We train our children to override their feelings and think in a linear fashion. Sometimes the correct decision does not come via a straight line or make sense at the time.

How many times did you just know something would work out? You trusted your intuition, and it felt right! When you override your instincts, you are giving your power away. We give in to authority too easily, and we are afraid to put ourselves out there. What will people think? What if I fail? What if people do not like me?

We are here to create. Our souls contain a unique thumbprint that is unlike anyone else in this Universe. It is your responsibility to leave your mark. Your mark is not your job. It is what makes you unique. Your uniqueness is what you do that feels easy and effortless and prompts people to ask, "How do you do that? You make that look so easy. I am always amazed at how you can do that so quickly."

"Remember that wherever your heart is, there you will find your treasure."
PAULO COELHO

I was recently on a business networking call for the Women in Oil and Gas Industry Association. A dynamic woman named Susan Morrice was on the call from Belize. She shared her story of fighting for her dream, believing in herself, and trusting her instincts. She told the story of stepping into her Truth.

Susan Morrice, an Irish woman, works for Belize Natural Energy (BNE), and she is a petroleum geoengineer. Her training in petroleum geoengineering convinced her Belize contained oil.

All of the major oil companies tried drilling oil there. Fifty different oil companies drilled fifty dry wells, and they all left believing Belize had no oil. Susan would not take no for an answer. She knew, deep in her heart and intuition, that there was oil. She visualized it before they began to drill.

She went home to Ireland and inspired people to invest in this little oil company. People mortgaged their homes and put all of their savings into her company. They raised one and a half million dollars, which at the time was considered by many to be a paltry sum for drilling oil.

Then a miracle happened. The first, second, and third wells they drilled all struck oil! Imagine an oil drilling bit the diameter of a dinner plate striking oil the first three times they drilled. It is literally like finding a needle in a haystack. Not only did they strike oil, but it was also so light that it did not require any refining.

Not only was Susan inspirational in finding the oil, she included the people of Belize in her efforts and set the standards so high they won a Green Award—the first and only oil company in the world to win a Green Award. They do not even have a refinery. Nature heats up the oil to forty degrees, and they only drilled thirty thousand feet. The oil goes direct without refining. The population of Belize is only four hundred thousand people, so Shell Oil Company buys what is left over. Susan made sure that the revenue went into their infrastructure, and her contributions to the local economy helped reduce crime by fifty percent.

When you are authentic, kind, passionate, and persistent, your dreams will come true. Susan's mission was not about the money. Her mission was about helping a country become energy independent, create jobs, and give power back to the citizens of Belize. Susan did not give up; she visualized and knew it was going to happen. She just needed to figure out how. When you remove the Lies and step into your Truth, you are unstoppable.[9]

---

[9] https://www.forbes.com/sites/rebeccaponton/2019/12/15/having-helped-discover-belizes-only-commercial-wells-susan-morrice-envisions-its-post-oil-future/?sh=1195b88828e8

We all have the ability to create what we want. Whatever you put your attention on grows, so put your attention on the solution. Sometimes the answer will show up in ways you least expect. There is no failure. If you want to manifest something, make sure you have an unshakable belief in what you want. No doubts. When you eliminate the beliefs that are not yours, when you know your values and live a life of integrity, you will discover a life of joy and happiness. Find your TRUTH, and you will never live a LIE.

Surrender, Faith, and Deep Trust That Everything Is in Universal Order

I have had a passion for travel ever since I was a young girl. I had been to Europe several times, but my ex-husband had not. When I realized that our twentieth wedding anniversary was coming up, I asked him how he felt about going on a trip to Europe? He said yes, but only if I was willing to do it on the back of a motorcycle. My ex-husband is passionate about motorcycles and is a competent driver, so I agreed. To determine a route that excited both of us, he suggested that we each take a few days and look up motorcycle-guided tours of Europe and check back to discuss what we had found.

Five years earlier, I was studying hypnosis. My instructor—who was psychic and very devoted to the Blessed Mother—gave me a message that I would travel to Bosnia and go to Medjugorje in May 2006. In this sacred place, Mother Mary appears as an apparition, and people experience spontaneous healings. According to the website medjugorje.org, "Since the apparitions began in 1981, over forty million people of all faiths, from all over the world, have visited Medjugorje and have left spiritually strengthened and renewed. Countless unbelievers and physically or mentally afflicted have been healed."

I am a firm believer in synchronicities, and this would end up being a big one in my life. As my ex and I began our search for motorcycle tours through Europe, he came home from a motorcycle rally, handed me a brochure and exclaimed, I found where we are going on our motorcycle trip, Croatia, Slovenia, and Bosnia!

How could this be? How did she possibly know the month and year I would be going to Bosnia exactly five years earlier? Not only that, but when she gave me the message, I told her that I was a Jewish girl from New Jersey. I asked her why she thought I would go to a place revered by Christians. On top of that, I knew Bosnia still had landmines.

My instructor looked at me, smiled, and said, "Of course, you are supposed to go. You do know that Mary was a Jewish mother, too, don't you? We both laughed out loud. I also had a very sick client who had always wanted to go, but he was too ill to travel. When I informed him that I was going to Medjugorje, he asked if I would go to the church, pray for him, and bring him back a set of rosary beads. I promised him that I would.

We arrived in Slovenia first, and I was immediately reminded of Vermont with its lush mountains and winding roads. Ten of us total were on the tour, including my cousins and a tour guide named Ishtock, who preferred us to call him Bambi for short. The owners of the tour company were a husband and wife team, and Martina, the wife, drove the van that carried our luggage and anyone who was too tired to ride or didn't want to get wet from the rain.

Each place we visited was more spectacular than the next. Croatia was breathtaking. We rode for about six hours per day, with stops every two hours. We stayed at little countryside inns, and every day offered new adventures. The people were wonderful, and our guides couldn't do enough for us.

As we got closer to Dubrovnik, our tour guide began to tell our group that Medjugorje was a tourist trap and there was nothing there to see. No one on our tour was in the least bit religious or spiritual, and none—other than me—had an interest in going. The group began planning to visit some really cool crater lakes in Croatia the next day instead.

This meant that my ex-husband and I would have to venture off on our own for the day if we were going to make it to Medjugorje. Since the GPS maps were not very accurate in 2006, and we couldn't read or speak the language, he began to get nervous about leaving the group. The night before we were supposed to go, he informed me that he wasn't comfortable taking me without a tour guide. It was all former Yugoslavia which was part of the old Soviet bloc, and no one spoke English. Not only did I feel that one of my purposes for being on the trip was visiting Medjugorje, but I also had a client who was depending on me to pray for him and bring him back rosary beads.

That night my ex and I got into a huge argument. I think the entire inn could hear us screaming at each other. I knew that he wanted to take me, but the logistics of going on our own seemed insurmountable to him. When I finally calmed down and crawled into bed, I said a prayer to the Blessed Mother and asked that if I was supposed to go to Medjugorje, please make it so. I prayed and asked that we would find the town easily and that our adventure would be comfortable and effortless. I made a list in my mind that included no crowds, and no buses, so he would feel at ease and safe along the way.

I was awakened at 5:00 the next morning, and my ex said that he had thought about it and that if it were that important to me, he would take me. Our tour guide told us that since we would be going on a slightly longer trip that day than the rest of the group, he recommended that we leave ahead of them, even though part of our journey would be the same.

I knew that my ex was uncomfortable, but I trusted that everything would happen for our highest and best. Of course, we had some trouble with the GPS immediately and missed the first turn. We only discovered it after going about fifteen minutes out of our way, and now we would be thirty minutes behind on our journey. We found a place to turn around, and as we came up to our exit on a major highway, we ran into Bambi, one of the guides on our tour. We couldn't believe our luck! He confirmed that this was the correct exit. He was standing by the exit sign waiting for the rest of the tour group. He had ridden ahead and decided to wait at the exit so no one would miss it. He waved us on, and we continued on our journey.

We decided to stop at a random café in the middle of a city that still showed remnants of the war. Bullet holes dotted the sides of buildings, yet the war had been over for ten years. It made me sad to think that the people lived with the constant reminders of war. We sat at the café, resting our aching behinds, having a drink, and then we heard the sound of motorcycles. We looked up, and the rest of our tour pulled up to the same cafe!

What are the chances of meeting up with them in the middle of a city? After our break, we rode together until it was time for us to split up, and we crossed the border into Bosnia. The language barrier was considerable. The letters were Cyrillic (Russian) and impossible for us to translate. My seven years of French in high school and college would not help me now.

We stopped for lunch at a café where we could not read the menu or communicate with the waiter. Luckily, they did understand the word pizza, but our waiter kept trying to find out what we wanted on our pizza. We laughed as we used hand gestures to describe the toppings that we were looking for. My ex said cheese and tomato sauce, you know, like ketchup. We were pleasantly surprised to receive a wonderful thin crust pizza with mushrooms on it and a side of ketchup in a bowl!

We had a great chuckle during lunch and continued on our route. There were very few cars on the road and no buses, just as I had prayed for! When we arrived in town, I was dropped off in front of the church, and he told me that I had thirty minutes. I got off the motorcycle in full motorcycle leathers, Frye boots, and a full-face helmet. I ran into the church and people began to stare at me, but I didn't care, I had made it!!!

I sat down in a pew, and suddenly the most incredible voice I had ever heard came out of a beautiful young woman. She was singing Ave Maria. It brought tears to my eyes. Even though I was not raised Christian, I could feel the love coming from the young woman while she sang. I started to feel light-headed and woozy. I stayed in my pew and took it all in. I closed my eyes and prayed for my clients, friends, and loved ones. I thanked the Blessed Mother Mary for guiding us and getting us to the church, and honoring my wishes. I also said a prayer thanking my ex-husband for offering to take me and going out of his comfort zone to make sure that we arrived at our destination. I contemplated the words channeled from my teacher five years before from Mother Mary and the grace that occurred to get me there.

The church was not crowded, and the streets were empty. It was not even close to the nightmare described to us. I finished my prayers in the church, and I ran into a storefront to grab a handful of rosary beads, cards, and gifts for friends and clients back home. I wanted to make sure that I was ready when it was time to leave. I finally caught up with my ex sitting in front of a gelato store, talking to a couple who told him about the crowds in Medjugorje and how the church had been so crowded that people were climbing over each other trying to get a seat in the pews. I was astonished because I found none of that.

We agreed that it was time to go, and the GPS suggested we take a back road rather than the way we originally came into town. We followed the new route, turned the corner, and neither of us could believe our eyes. Thousands of people were coming toward us. It was a sea of people headed right at us and buses everywhere! We had to squeeze through masses of people, double-decker buses, wheelchairs, and people being carried because they were too sick to walk. The buses were from many different countries, and we could hear several different languages being spoken. All who arrived had hope in their hearts for miracles in their life. Some came for physical healing, some for emotional healing, and others for the opportunity to possibly see the Blessed Mother appear. So many people had a look of desperation in their eyes, and yet others were filled with pure joy at the idea of arriving at this sacred place.

After what seemed an eternity, we finally got past the mass of people, and suddenly, the GPS told us to take a U-turn, leading us back to the front of the church. We looked at each other. My ex wondered what that was all about and wanted to know why the GPS put us through that unbelievable maze of people. I believe that we were being shown the miracle of that day. Everything I prayed for happened and my heart was overcome with joy. I realized that I was bringing home hope to a few special people back home—whether they were going to receive a physical healing or not.

I gave a set of rosary beads to my client, who kept them with him at all times. He would go into a panic if he put them down and couldn't find them. He told me how the beads helped him and gave him peace during radiation and chemotherapy. He thanked me for the gift and told me how much the beads meant to him and how he loved holding them in his hands. Unfortunately, his illness got the best of him, and after a long, painful battle, he passed on. I attended his wake, and as I prayed by his casket, I looked down and saw the rosary beads from Medjugorje in his hands. My heart swelled, and tears welled up in my eyes.

As we finally left Medjugorje, I thanked my ex-husband for his willingness to go and told him how much I appreciated that he went out of his comfort zone to take me. We continued on our journey to Dubrovnik to meet up with the rest of our group. We ended up on one of the most beautiful roads I have ever traveled in my life. It was narrow and carved carefully into the mountains. The road consisted of very sharp switchback turns. We grew tired and saw a little inn on the side of the road and decided to stop for a drink. We walked inside, and there was the rest of our tour group! After hours of being separated and in two different countries, we caught up with them at a random inn in the middle of nowhere!

I share that story because I have found that in my life, when I am presented with options and opportunities that push me out of my comfort zone, I have learned to say yes, surrender, and trust. I searched for my Truth, and my Truth appeared that day. Sometimes when it appears that things are not going my way, they end up being the best-case scenario. By trusting that the Universe is conspiring for you, you can surrender and allow circumstances to happen and trust that lessons will appear. Eliminating the Lies in your beliefs allows you to create your dreams. I trusted and *knew* at a deep level that if I was meant to go to Medjugorje, it would happen. I had no idea when I went to bed what the outcome would be in the morning when I awoke.

Oftentimes we can be attached to what something needs to look like, but the better option is the one you would never have considered. Just because I surrender does not mean I am free from difficulties and struggles or that I give up and just let things happen to me. Sometimes I am guided to take the harder road for a lesson that I need to experience. I may not even know what the lesson was at the time. I will just go with the feeling that guides me on my way. Lessons do not come in a straight line. Taking the road less traveled is often the greatest gift you can give yourself.

Here is a famous parable I love. It really demonstrates the ability to be neutral and to trust.

A farmer and his son had a beloved horse who helped the family earn a living. One day, the horse ran away, and their neighbors exclaimed, "Your horse ran away; what terrible luck!" The farmer replied, "Maybe so, maybe not."

A few days later, the horse returned home, leading a few wild horses back to the farm as well. The neighbors shouted out, "Your horse has returned, and brought several horses home with him. What great luck!" The farmer replied, "Maybe so, maybe not."

Later that week, the farmer's son was trying to break one of the horses, and she threw him to the ground, breaking his leg. The neighbors cried, "Your son broke his leg; what terrible luck!" The farmer replied, "Maybe so, maybe not."

A few weeks later, soldiers from the national army marched through town, recruiting all boys for the army. They did not take the farmer's son because he had a broken leg. The neighbors shouted, "Your boy is spared; what tremendous luck!" To which the farmer replied, "Maybe so, maybe not. We'll see."

You see the world through your own lens. You have a choice as to how you want to interpret it. You can also set the tone of your day every morning when you wake up. You can choose to be happy, grumpy, angry, impatient, joyful, empowered, or a victim. When you live a Lie, choices are hard because that belief is programmed into you, and it can be hard to change. When you live in your Truth, it's easier for you to set the intention to have a joyful, loving, wonderful experience—even if it is a mundane or bad day. Many people would tell you how they would pray for one of your mundane days.

> *"I enjoy life when things are happening. I don't care if it's good or bad things. That means you're alive."*
> *Joan Rivers*

If you look at everything from a state of wonder, grace, and enchantment, your days will always feel magical. If something happens that you perceive to be bad, tell yourself there is a reason for this, and something great will happen because of it. I have no idea what that is, but I will trust that the answer will come one day. Unfortunately, many of us do not automatically walk around with happiness as our default. However, we can choose to start our day with gratitude and hope.

Exercise

When you wake up in the morning, look at everything with childlike wonder. As if you are seeing everything for the first time. Look at the sunrise, cherish your cup of coffee and drink it slowly, take time to meditate and reflect on the things that bring you joy. Say yes to things that take you out of your comfort zone. Make note of how your day went and if you felt a difference.

Chapter 12

Tools That Help Transform Your Lies Into Your Truth!

One day I was watching someone talk about being in the present moment and I became very frustrated. I desperately wanted him to show me how to become present. So many experts talk about being in the present moment, but I had no idea what that meant and what it could possibly look like. I recently had a teacher tell me that the present is one full breath in and out. He told me that in order to be present, you need to slow down. When you are present, you are a creator. Your mind begins to use your imagination and you start to create things, you manifest. When you go too fast, you are actually becoming like a robot. You are reacting instead of creating. Many of us think that we need to stay busy all of the time and get lots of things accomplished. When you do that, you are not present and you feel exhausted. It actually takes more energy to be busy reacting than it does to be present and create.

When you are present, focus on what you want to attract. The Universe will respond to your thoughts and emotions. The stronger your thoughts and emotions are, the faster you will manifest your desires. I make a habit of visualizing, feeling and experiencing what I want in my mind every morning when I wake up and when I get into bed at night. If your subconscious mind is clear about what you want and there are no negative beliefs or lies blocking you, you will begin to attract what you desire.

Don't forget that the Universe does not know negatives. According to Don Miguel Ruiz, author of the "The Four Agreements", the first agreement is to be impeccable with your word. You create and manifest everything through your word. Your word is magic. You can create pure magic or black magic by saying positive things or negative things. Gossip, judging, and negative talk about someone is harmful not only to the person you are talking about, but it also comes back to harm you, which prevents you from manifesting. When you stay in fear and anger, it will block manifestation and give you exactly what you don't want. When you forgive, it purifies your energy field and things begin to flow to you easily and effortlessly.

Here are some tools that I use to help slow down and become more present. Tools

Smile: Did you know that when you smile, even if it is fake, your brain will produce a cascade of neuropeptides and release endorphins like dopamine and serotonin? The result is a decrease in pain and stress and a boost to your immune system. Remember, your subconscious mind does not know the difference between reality and a movie. Fake it until you make it. Not only will you feel better, but smiles are also infectious. When you start smiling, others around you will start smiling too.

Music is a powerful healer. Music can transport you to a memory. It can create a mood. It can make you cry or bring you to your feet to dance. I thought about the song "Smile" by Nat King Cole, and if you read the lyrics, he confirms that just pretending to smile will bring you joy. When I read the lyrics, it brought a smile to my face. If you enjoy them, consider printing them and keeping them nearby to cheer you up. Enjoy!

Lisa Schermerhorn

"Smile"
by Nat King Cole

Smile though your heart is aching
Smile even though it's breaking
When there are clouds in the sky, you'll get by
If you smile through your fear and sorrow
Smile and maybe tomorrow
You'll see the sun come shining through for you
Light up your face with gladness
Hide every trace of sadness
Although a tear may be ever so near
That's the time you must keep on trying
Smile, what's the use of crying?
You'll find that life is still worthwhile
If you just smile
That's the time you must keep on trying
Smile, what's the use of crying?
You'll find that life is still worthwhile
If you just smile

Source: LyricFind
Songwriters: Charles Chaplin / Geoffrey Parsons /
John Turner

Breathe: Did you realize that breath is life? When you breathe deeply from your lower abdomen, you tug on the parasympathetic nervous system, which stimulates the vagus nerve, lowering your heart rate and reducing anxiety. You can use this breathing technique with a slow deep intentional breath. Try counting to six while breathing in, holding your breath for a count of three, exhaling for six, and holding for three. If you do this for just a few minutes—at any time of day or multiple times a day—you will find a vast difference in how you feel. You can use this technique for meditation. I will generally set my timer on my phone for ten minutes if I don't have much time to meditate. Close your office door or go outside; find a quiet place and breathe for a few minutes.

Meditate: Information about the benefits of meditation is abundant. I often hear, "I don't have time; my mind races too much; I don't know how." If you know how to breathe, you can meditate. If you sit straight up, set your timer for ten minutes on your phone, and breathe deeply, you are meditating. Meditation has been scientifically proven to improve your immune system, reduce stress, increase empathy, alleviate depression, lower blood pressure, increase productivity, and promote creative thinking. This is just the beginning! Meditation offers so many benefits, and it changed my life.

Often people think that they are being most productive when they are working and doing something. Yet, have you experienced an aha moment while your mind is quiet? When I meditate, my creativity soars; so many ideas arise seemingly from nowhere. Meditation is part of my daily ritual. Ten minutes will give you great benefits. Everyone has ten minutes. Countless apps offer guided meditations if you aren't comfortable with meditating quietly. Everyone has to start somewhere. It will not always be smooth sailing, but the more consistent you are, the more benefits you will experience. Rather than focusing on quieting your mind, try observing your thoughts, and notice the inspiration that comes.

Let it go: Several years ago, I learned a technique called the Emotional Release Method. My mentor Dr. Al taught me these tools, and he spent hours helping me release old beliefs and wounds I was still holding on to. I learned to surrender and believe that everything is in divine order. I use this method almost every day and share it with all of my clients. This is an incredibly powerful technique that I use almost every day for myself and my clients. Focus on the feeling in your body, rank it from one to ten, ten being the highest. Focus on that feeling and repeat the following mantra until the number on the scale is zero or you feel neutral:

Should I let it go? Yes!
Could I let it go? Yes!
When? Now!

Emotional Freedom Technique: This technique, also known as EFT, is another amazing technique I have discovered. EFT can be used for physical pain and emotional distress. It is also referred to as tapping. People who use this technique believe tapping on specific parts of the body creates a balance in your energy system. I have found this technique is just as powerful as the Emotional Release Method, but this involves a sequence of tapping on your meridians and releasing blocks that have been stored in your thoughts and your body for years. When the Sandy Hook shooting tragedy happened, Nick, Jessica, and Alex Ortner gathered with the victims of the shooting and taught them EFT to help them find some peace. They established the Tapping Solution Foundation along with Dr. Lori Leyden, Founder of Create Global Healing. If you are interested in finding out more, visit www.tappingsolutionfoundation.com. Many other organizations teach and offer EFT as well.

Eye Movement Release Technique: This technique, also known as EMRT, was created by Kevin Martin. This technique has been proven to massively decrease emotional triggers, reduce emotional pain, eliminate cravings, and more. The technique consists of a simple eye movement that often works immediately. If you want to know more, contact Kevin Martin at www.peakperformancemindsetcoaching.com

Hypnosis: I owe a lot to hypnosis; it changed my life. Many people have a negative connotation of it because of stage hypnotists, which is a very different form of hypnosis. I do not know how to entertain people in a crowd. My work is primarily one-to-one, and I cannot make people do anything they do not want to do. You allow yourself to be hypnotized, and I say allow because the individual is in charge. If you do not want to be hypnotized, you will not be. Hypnosis allows people to explore thoughts, feelings, and memories they may have hidden from their consciousness. We all naturally go in and out of hypnosis seven to ten times per day. If you have ever daydreamed, meditated, passed an exit while driving, or arrived at a destination and you do not really remember how you got there, you were in a state of hypnosis, which is just considered an altered brain wave state. That's it. During hypnosis, you are completely aware of what is going on, and you have control of what happens.

Neuro-Linguistic Programming: This technique, also known as NLP, is considered the study of excellence. According to Tony Robbins, it is a tool for those interested in personal growth. NLP techniques are useful for creating rapport, increasing sales, team building and building leadership skills. NLP can be used alone or with other types of therapy. Part of NLP is learning to discover your map of the world, your lens, and what created your internal programming. It's incredibly powerful and can be used to change lives.

These tools are just a few of many that can be used to help you uncover your false beliefs. Your Lies. Remember that when we are lying to ourselves, our beliefs reinforce those thoughts and then we act on them, even when they are false. Changing your Lies will change your life.

If you are looking for more tools to help you release the Lies and live your Truth, use this QR Code to take you to several videos demonstrating and explaining the tools in a deeper way and some guided meditations to help you shift and enhance the changes you have already made.

Chapter Thirteen

Conclusion

My aspiration for you in reading this book was to give you hope, show you it is possible to live a joyful life, have the courage to go after your dreams, and take back your power in order to live your Truth.

My path on this journey was not easy, but I never felt I had a different choice. In the beginning, though, I simply didn't know where to go. When I began my journey twenty years ago, I searched to find my Truth. I kept praying for help, and I was looking for someone to hold my hand and show me the answers. I worked with a lot of teachers and really brilliant mentors.

Along the way, people would ask me, "Lisa, why are you taking another class? You already have everything you need." I never understood that perspective because I always believed that the answers would come from outside of me. Since I didn't know who I was, I would let others tell me who I was and how to accomplish my goals. I had accumulated so many Lies that I couldn't imagine that I could have the answers deep inside of me.

It reminds me of Dorothy in the Wizard of Oz. She went on an incredible journey to find her way home, and in the end, she had the power to get home all along, but she didn't know it. Throughout my long inner journey, my goal was to become the person I was searching for who would provide me with all of the answers and tell me what to do. I finally realized that it would never happen until I discarded all of the Lies I told myself.

When we discover our Lies—the programming that doesn't belong to us—and let them go, it frees us up to discover our Truth. When I stopped looking outside of myself and started trusting my decisions fully and completely, my life changed. When I gave up the need to worry, my focus and attention were no longer preoccupied with looking for everything that could possibly go wrong. I could focus on my dreams, what I wanted, and visualize my future. I no longer stress and freak out over something that may never happen.

The irony is that when you get rid of your Lies, you'll find a period when you may experience nothingness. For me, it felt disconcerting at first. The more I trusted the feeling and understood that I was learning a new way to navigate the world, the more I surrendered to it. The quieter I got, the louder my old Lies would appear. I would observe them and let them go. When the Lies began to diminish, I began to feel peace.

That doesn't mean that everything is perfect and I don't have any problems. I am human and still deal with complicated issues regularly, but the difference is that I don't get caught up in drama anymore. I don't let the little wounded girl inside me make my decisions anymore.

When you quiet the mind, spend time alone in nature, and allow yourself to be at peace, that is where the magic happens. That is where the gold is stored. People think they need to be productive and busy all of the time, and work has to be hard. It doesn't mean that I am saying not to work hard, but when I work, it doesn't feel like work; it feels joyful, purposeful, and meaningful. When you know your Why, your values, your purpose, and release the Lies, you are given the freedom and the gift of your Truth, and when you live your Truth, you exercise your free will.

One of my clients is a consultant, and he achieved a financial level he never dreamed he would reach. Then suddenly, it seemed all of his clients dried up overnight. He was stressed and frustrated because he was waiting for his clients to get back to him about moving forward on some really important projects. The Lie he held was that the clients were in charge. We reframed the situation, so he realized that they were actually waiting for him since he was the expert. Since he knew his worth, he would charge accordingly and give a lot of value and show them how he could make their businesses more profitable and their lives better. He realized that by living his Truth and eliminating the Lies that he created, he discovered that he was creating his own destiny and freedom.

Are you ready for freedom? Are you ready to release your Lies?

If you are looking for a deeper dive and are ready to discover your Truth, contact me through my website www.peakperformancemindsetcoaching.com.

I offer group and VIP coaching that will help you transform your life and get you to where you want to be. I know that time is precious in this crazy world, and I know you have a lot of competition for your time. I am truly honored that you have taken time out of your busy schedule to read this book. If you found this book valuable, please share it with a friend. The more people we help, the more joy we spread.

The End

About the Author

Lisa Schermerhorn

Lisa has over twenty years of experience as a transformational leader, award-winning speaker, and international best-selling author expert in the fields of human behavior, leadership, and personal development. She also trained in the "Winners Mindset" with Bob Reese, the former head trainer for the New York Jets, and helped a professional golfer win Golfer of the Year!

Lisa was Vice President of Business Development for an innovative start-up company using virtual reality to help clients reduce pain, memory loss, and stress. As a Certified Hypnotherapist and Master Practitioner of Neuro-Linguistic Programming (NLP), she helps entrepreneurs and high performers achieve their goals by helping them get from where they are to where they want to be much faster than conventional coaches.

Lisa is also trained as a Why Coach, helping people discover their Why, based on Simon Sinek's *Know Your Why*. Lisa helps individuals discover their personal

Why, and she also helps people discover the Why of their business and how to use it effectively in branding.

Lisa lives with her dog Lily who she rescued at the age of ten from a high-kill shelter. Please consider adopting a senior dog and saving a life.

Can You Help My Mom?

Thank You For Reading My Mom's Book!

My mom really appreciates all of your feedback, and we love hearing what you have to say.

She needs your input to make the next version of this book and her future books better.

Please leave her an honest review on Amazon letting her know what you thought of the book.

Thanks so much!

Lily

35469403R00104